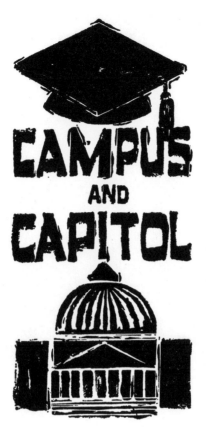

CAMPUS AND CAPITOL

HIGHER EDUCATION AND THE STATE /
Papers from the Eighth Annual College Self
Study Institute / July 11-14, 1966 / University
of California / Berkeley / Sponsored by the
Western Interstate Commission for Higher Edu-
cation and the Center for Research and De-
velopment in Higher Education, University of
California, Berkeley.

College Self Study Institute, 8th

W. John Minter

Editor

Western Interstate Commission for Higher Education
University East Campus, Boulder, Colorado 80302
November, 1966

Additional copies available. $3.50

Preface

The Western Interstate Commission for Higher Education and the Center for Research and Development in Higher Education, Berkeley, present here the papers of the Eighth Annual College Self Study Institute. Since 1960, the Commission has joined with the Center to co-sponsor institutes in a number of areas of interest to administrators in higher education.

It is appropriate that an agency of the states and a center for scholarly research join in sponsoring a discussion of higher education and the state. WICHE and the Center are proud to bring this material to the educators and legislators of the West.

Leland L. Medsker, Acting Chairman
Center for Research and Development in
Higher Education

Robert H. Kroepsch, Executive Director
Western Interstate Commission for
Higher Education

November, 1966
Boulder, Colorado

Contents

Introduction

One purpose of the institute and these papers is to furnish information for the debate which will be vigorously pursued as educators and legislators find their concerns becoming more and more intertwined. We agree with Sam Gould who points out that much of the vital dialogue cannot be, and should not be, reduced to manuscript. These papers, however, do identify important issues and values which must be weighed carefully by both educators and legislators as they seek to discharge their particular responsibilities in the public interest. We commend them to you for what thought, discussion, and research they may stimulate.

What are the most important dimensions of the growing interdependence between government and higher education? That was the basic question for study at the Eighth Annual College Self Study Institute. One concern was the federal government. How has the relationship between federal government and higher education been modified by recent legislative action? What appear to be the long-term trends in this relationship of growing interdependence? These questions were asked in an effort to assess the impact of federal legislation on the university campus.

But there are fifty state capitols. What of their interest in higher education? Comparatively little research has been published in this area. Therefore, the planning committee invited several speakers to address themselves to such questions as: What are the appropriate roles of governors and legislators, vis-a-vis governing boards when developing institutional, fiscal, and educational policy? What practical steps might be taken to develop more effective collaboration between state government and higher education? What important influences are shaping current patterns of state-wide coordination and cooperation? What are the meanings of institutional autonomy and institutional identity? By what means can institutional autonomy and institutional identity be appropriately maintained in a state coordinated system?

A recent event of particular concern to the higher education community was the organization of the Compact for Education. What appear to be the most important implications of the compact for the governance of higher education? Will the compact affect private and public higher institutions alike? What dimensions of institutional autonomy may be threatened by the compact? This new interstate compact, embracing all levels of education and the executive and legislative branches of state governments, illustrates the growing involvement of elected officials in educational policy.

Why should universities be free from government interference and restrictive controls? What key issues are at stake when governments exercise close budgetary controls over higher institutions? What is an appropriate division of fiscal responsibility between government agencies and university trustees? How have foreign governments and systems of higher education handled these issues? These and other fundamental questions close the discussion for this institute.

W. John Minter
Institute Director

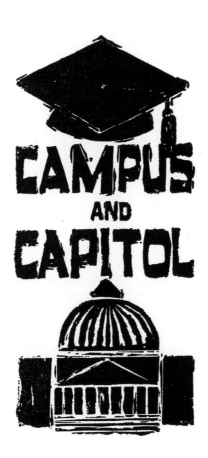

CAMPUS
AND
CAPITOL

Precis
The University and State Government:
Fears and Realities

The realistic circumstance here is that full and unreserved public discussion of the relations between a university and state government could have the effect of straining and weakening the very elements such a discussion is intended to strengthen. The more subtle personal contacts which are the warp and woof of the fabric of this relationship defy rules and definitions and formulas. They differ in every single instance, even though they are the true means by which the delicate balance of authority, responsibility, and interdependence existing between the university and state government is maintained, or, when matters go awry, is upset.

The first reality in our relationship with state government is the degree of our own faith in the democratic process and our belief in those, regardless of party affiliation, who are the elected representatives of the people in promulgating that process.

An all-encompassing reality is clear. Adherence to the advocacy of an expanding system of public higher education has now become one of the most popular positions in current political life. A new set of attitudes is emerging in many of our states, based upon a desire, first, to know the facts about higher education, and second, to do what appears appropriate in light of these facts. The problem and danger, however, occur when the questioning of committees and governmental staffs reaches into areas of academic competence and scholarly judgment.

The erosion of the independence of a university can begin in what may seem rather trivial specifics at the moment of their occurrence. The heart of the matter, therefore, is our readiness to recognize and defend the portion of our institutional life and development which is not within the bailiwick of anyone else to prescribe or control or even touch. Any evaluation of state government-university relationships should start with an examination of how well and in what formal terms the protection of this portion of institutional life is provided. If we have fears, and most of us do, they center upon this point.

The public universities of today and tomorrow, then, should have their basic freedom of action guaranteed to them by constitutional authority, yet seek to create a climate of understanding and trust which will make recourse to legal defenses unnecessary in all but the most extraordinary circumstances.

Chapter 1

The University and State Government: Fears and Realities

by
Samuel B. Gould
President
State University of New York

Unless my judgment is completely erroneous, this conference will be looked upon in retrospect as being unique in at least *one* way: it will be remembered more for what is *not* said than for what *is* said. Or, to qualify this statement somewhat, it will be remembered more for what is said in the corridors than from the platform. But then, perhaps this is not unique, after all; many of us can recall numerous conferences where this was so. The difference comes in the conference subject. The realistic circumstance here is that full and unreserved public discussion of the relations between a university and state government could have the effect of straining and weakening the very elements such a discussion is intended to strengthen. In addition, the whole subject is surrounded by a sense of fear and hesitancy that tends to becloud the realities.

I do not mean to give the impression by what I have just said that ultra-mysterious and darkly nefarious activities take place in university-state government relations. On the contrary, whatever does happen in the establishment of policies or the results of such policies is open and free to scrutinize. It would be illegal or unscrupulous to have it otherwise. But the more subtle personal contacts which are the warp and woof of the fabric of this relationship defy rules and definitions and formulas. They differ in every single instance, even though they are the true means by which the delicate balance of authority, responsibility, and interdependence existing between the university and state government is maintained, or, when matters go awry, is upset. They represent the interplay of personalities, the development of attitudes on the part of these personalities reflecting a clear understanding of respective roles and motivations, and most of all the creation of a climate of mutual trust and respect.

Let me pause for a moment on this last point because I believe it to be extremely important, so important that without our agreement upon it the entire conference could degenerate into a study of artfully manipulative techniques. If such were indeed to be the case, it would be a major tragedy and a permanently lost opportunity.

Politicians and Educators: Differing Ways and Responsibilities

The first responsibility we have as educational administrators about to approach the process of dealing with the executive and legislative branches of state government is that of understanding, having sympathy for, and respecting the practical elements of political life. The ways of men elected to political office and the kinds of burdens they bear are not *our* ways or *our* burdens. They are part of the democratic pattern and they will always be present. Furthermore, they are necessary.

It is essential that we do not fall into the easy and dangerous trap of beginning our considerations of state government relationships from the premise that men in political office are crassly motivated, are intellectually inferior, and never rise above party loyalties. The stigma all too often attached to the term "politician" and the characteristics attributed to such a person, which have unfortunately become part of the mythology of our country, are generalizations unworthy of us all. We in the academic world have done little to counteract that stigma or to destroy that myth; indeed, we have oftentimes encouraged them. There are charlatans and hacks in political life, to be sure; there are charlatans and hacks in academic life as well, and we should look well and deeply into our own profession before we adopt a posture of superiority to any other.

I find that, in the main, people in the executive and legislative branches of state government are greatly concerned about the

4

welfare of their total constituencies, just as we are. They are hard-working men and women who emerge remarkably well from the effects of the multiplicity of pressures placed upon them by every segment of our society, including our own. They make mistakes just as we do; they are sometimes misled and misinformed like the rest of us. But the progress of most states, whether in health, social reforms, education, conservation of resources, transportation, and all the rest, is unmistakable to us all. And the executive and legislative leadership is the prime factor in this progress.

Whatever we, as educational leaders, intend to accomplish as our part in assisting the process of progress within our states can be done only with a full realization that government is bound to be involved in our efforts. Our task, therefore, is to develop personal relationships which make it possible for us to make clear to men in government the nature of our enterprise, the role we ourselves play, the portion of our institutional life and development which is not within the bailiwick of anyone else to prescribe or control or even touch, and most of all, the heavy responsibility resting upon *them* as well as upon *us* in fulfilling the education of our youth and, indeed, the total citizenry. It must be made equally clear that we and they have an unusual partnership in all this, the kind of partnership that gives to each side a specific set of assignments to be fulfilled in the interests of expanding and improving higher education.

The first reality in our relationship with state government is the degree of our own faith in the democratic process and our belief in those, regardless of party affiliation, who are the elected representatives of the people in promulgating that process.

New York State and the State University

In the course of examining a few more of the fears and realities of university-state government relationships, perhaps it would be helpful if I explained rather specifically the role of the governor and that of the legislature in New York as they pertain to the university. Such roles may differ in your own respective states, yet I should imagine there are basic similarities.

The State Executive and SUNY

The influence of the governor of New York upon educational and fiscal policy in public higher education is perhaps greater than any single force external to the university itself. He has the power,

5

first of all, to appoint all fifteen members of the Board of Trustees. It is possible that this power can be used to the detriment of the university. In actuality, however, the constructive way this power has been exercised is best evidenced by the strong, loyal, and dedicated service these good citizens perform in the interests of the university, all without any signs of political partisanship.

The governor's influence over the budget of the university and in the allocation of the state's tax resources to the many competing claims upon the budget is perhaps his most significant power. The budget director and his staff, acting in behalf of the governor, are in a constant and continuing year-round relationship to the university. This provides them with an opportunity to assess and evaluate our performance, to be sure, but it also affords us the equally important opportunity to orient them to the values, standards, needs, and aspirations of a university as these differ from those of regular government departments.

The university is required by statute to submit, every four years through the Board of Regents to the governor for his approval, a master plan covering the next ten years. It must also submit annual amendments to this plan. Here is an example of the governor's influence upon educational policy generally. This kind of power makes possible the virtual vetoing of specific programs for the creation of new institutions, the inauguration of new major academic programs, changes in orientation and emphasis, and the like. Another example of such influence is the governor's power to review (or later veto) legislation which the university wishes to introduce in the legislature. His willingness to give approval may help in a friendly legislature; his unwillingness may place the university in an awkward position in determining whether it should seek to introduce such legislation on its own behalf on the chance that he would not veto it once passed by the legislature. His endorsement in a hostile legislature may be fatal. In a divided legislature, which almost always demands compromise for any effective action, the degree to which he becomes active in behalf of the university is the determinant of success or failure.

The Legislature and SUNY

The influence of the legislature tends to be less well defined and less specific than that of the governor. With many members having generally shorter terms and being more subject to change, and with much shorter periods of time annually in the state capitol, their powers, while concentrated during a session, give the impression of being less pervasive and continuing. They ordinarily initiate less than do governors.

Yet, their powers are great. They can give expanded authority; they can take it away. They can cut budgets; they can increase them. They can investigate and chart new paths of constructive legislative enactment; they can also investigate and destroy. They can reach into public higher education and force additions to the master plan; they can curtail enrollments; they can even create new professorial chairs on their own recognizance.

Even the simple recounting of executive and legislative power and influence is enough to raise many questions about what is to be feared or what is actual reality. There is no doubt that the university would have much to fear if it thought only of the legally designated powers which could be exerted upon it externally. But there is also no doubt that there are offsetting realities against which these fears can be placed and which give cause for at least a certain amount of optimism.

The Popular Position is to Expand Education

One of the all-encompassing realities is clear. Adherence to the advocacy of an expanding system of public higher education has now become one of the most popular positions in current political life. I am speaking of the situation in many states, not merely of New York. The tremendous surge in the numbers of college-age youth coupled with the ever-growing needs for trained manpower and retrained manpower has made political leaders aware more than ever before of the close relationship between a strong economy and a highly educated citizenry. Added to this are new realizations of what increased leisure time will mean in the future and how citizens must be prepared for this leisure, of what it means to have youth leave the state for want of adequate educational opportunity, and of what cultural responsibilities and opportunities are now coming to the forefront of community attention.

These developments combine to make a political platform in favor of expanded higher education most attractive to any candidate or any office incumbent. A flood of letters from constituents complaining because their sons and daughters can find no place for themselves in the state's academic institutions, or a series of petitions from professional and technical groups pointing to shortages of skilled personnel and asking bluntly what training programs are in prospect to alleviate these shortages can soon sharpen the sensitivity of the legislator and stir his feeling of personal responsibility. Beyond this is the deep conviction held by many in public life that the true measure of our democracy is identified in our ability to educate to the limit of their potential all who are qualified.

Knowledge for Sound Judgments

We see a new set of attitudes emerging in many of our states, based upon a desire, first, to know the facts about higher education, and second, to do what appears appropriate in light of these facts. Governors are identifying themselves with the cause of higher education as never before. Legislatures are setting up joint committees of one sort or another backed up by permanent professional staffs in order to acquire full knowledge and to meet the problems of higher education with intelligent and careful judgment. Through such committees a university has an opportunity to be heard on major matters of public educational policy and to interpret its own needs and aspirations. With pressures for change and growth as they are today, unless a university seizes upon this opportunity, it will soon find legislative committees doing the interpretation themselves. (And, as an aside, may I say that when a university goes about interpreting its missions, it must do so in language understandable to the legislator, not in the academic jargon which sometimes fills our catalogues and other public pronouncements.)

Theoretically and ideally, I suppose one might take the position that universities should have none but the most nominal relationships with any bodies of state government. They should merely specify what they require and be given it with no questions asked. But such an ideal has rarely, if ever, existed anywhere, and it is certainly not likely to come into existence today. The very reverse is true. The huge amounts of money necessary for all of us to carry on make the governors and legislators and even the taxpayers all the more curious about how these monies are expended. And if all their curiosity concentrates upon the kind of stewardship of funds we maintain, or the safeguards we use to assure everyone that money is being used appropriately and economically, or the results of all this expenditure in terms of the quality of our academic results, there is no reason to complain. We are not such a mysterious or esoteric priesthood that we cannot and should not provide such information willingly and even eagerly.

Who Makes the Judgments?

The problem and the danger begin to grow more acute, however, when the questioning of committees and governmental staffs reaches into areas of academic competence and scholarly judgment. Who is to decide, for example, what are the appropriate faculty-student ratios for instruction? Who is to decide the priorities by which a university is to achieve its various missions as they relate to intellectual life generally and to service needs of the state? Who is to make judgments about matters of academic freedom? Who is to determine where new campuses or institutions are to be situated? We could form a long list of such questions, but they all add up to the necessity for constant alertness on our part and unequivocal opposition when educational questions begin to be answered with political solutions.

The heart of the matter, therefore, is our readiness to recognize and defend what I defined earlier as "the portion of our institutional life and development which is not within the bailiwick of anyone else to prescribe or control or even touch." Any evaluation of state government-university relationships should start with an examination of how well and in what formal terms the protection of this portion of institutional life is provided. In repeating what I defined, let me emphasize the phrase "*in formal terms.*" If we have fears (and most of us do), they center upon this point.

Erosion of Institutional Independence

The erosion of the independence of a university can begin in what may seem rather trivial specifics at the moment of their occurrence. Each one of these probably touches upon some aspect of university independence incompletely understood by the external person or agency. In most instances, appropriate discussion and explanation may clear up the misunderstanding and cause rescinding of the action, but the vulnerability of the university remains. And if the action is not altered and the pressure withdrawn, a precedent has been set which can lead to similar actions as a regular pattern, actions which can gradually begin to deal with far less trivial matters. A complete and sympathetic understanding by *one* budget director does not guarantee a similar attitude on the part of the next; careful avoidance of dictation in academic affairs by *one* legislative committee is no assurance of what the next will do. And no matter how assiduously we try to develop processes of orientation for newly appointed or elected officials, such processes are long and tedious, and much happens in the meantime.

Examples of Erosion at State Institutions

I could offer typical examples of the eroding specifics to which I am referring, and I am certain you have at least as many of your own that you could supply. Some tend to influence policy-making by boards of trustees; some reflect attempts at fiscal control that come close to directing decisions on academic activities and curricular change; some illustrate the seizure of initiative by a governmental agency in shaping the university's academic plans. All of them have elements of actual or potential danger, and we must be alert to what they could presage for the future.

Let me illustrate a few of these; even though they are presumably suppositions, as we would all like to feel, they *could* happen. Each represents the start of a tendency toward outside dictation which, if unchecked, could have anything but trivial consequences:

1. A legislator expounds in the public press his doubts about the wisdom of a university decision regarding the site of a new campus, giving unmistakable signs that he expects such a decision to take into account political considerations for the region rather than educational ones.

2. A directive (usually verbal) comes from a staff member in the executive chamber indicating that purchase of certain kinds of specialized equipment is to be cleared with him.

3. A legislative committee eliminates certain academic positions relating to a previously approved academic program on the grounds that their own judgment on the way the program is to be developed is the ruling one.

4. Funds for a minor week-end conference of staff or faculty are withheld on a pre-audit basis with the explanation that university personnel should pay their own expenses in such instances.

5. A legislator asks that a full disclosure be made by the university of the reasons why a particular faculty member has not received a renewal of his term appointment.

6. A committee is recommended to the legislature for the purpose of maintaining surveillance over students and faculty as to actions that might be interpreted as subversive because they reflect unpopular or unorthodox attitudes and opinions.

We could multiply such examples manyfold in their type and variety if we were to examine the experience of universities all over this country. They are becoming *more* prevalent rather than less.

Independent University or Public Agency?

Another element of erosion stems from the assumption by some state government executives and legislators that a public university is no more than another branch of state government, with exactly the same status as any government agency and therefore subject to exactly the same regulations. Indeed, the most difficult problem some of us may have is that of persuading state officials and the citizenry in general that it is absolutely essential that a university, if it is to be worthy of the name, is not at all the same as a government agency. And if it is forced to operate inflexibly under the rules of a government agency, it is doomed to mediocrity or worse.

This is not to urge for university authority and independence without responsibility. It is rather to recognize the differences between a university and state departmental agencies because of their differences in purpose and mission. It is to recognize the necessity for freeing the university from as many bureaucratic strictures as are feasible in order that it may take the appropriate initiative in developing and transforming itself to meet the needs of the times and the society it serves.

Have Universities Abdicated Initiative?

In the matter of establishing firmly where initiative for university development should originate, we of the academic world have already exhibited numerous forms of intellectual flabbiness and academic rationalization. Far too many grants from foundations eager to assist the progress of education have come about not because a university has thought through a new pattern or an innovative approach, but rather because foundation staff themselves have wanted to test certain theories. The university has many times accepted such assistance eagerly for prestige reasons and for the money itself. In the past few years the federal government has taken on the same role as the foundations with even greater temp-

11

tations to the universities, temptations to which we react in accordance with Oscar Wilde's famous dictum, namely, that "the only way to get rid of a temptation is to yield to it."

This is not to be critical of either the foundations or the federal government for their motives, which reflect a desire to do something better than it has been done. It is, rather, to point out that not enough initiative for such improvement seems to come from universities themselves, even when they know funds are possibly available. People removed from university life are doing the planning in very specific ways and are forcing the issues to conclusions which may or may not fit in with the institution's original objectives.

In recent months we have had another initiating agent introduced into the picture in the form of the new Compact of the States. Here is a new instrument heavily weighted on the governmental side, with excellent objectives in terms of gathering and disseminating information, but with another potentiality for transferring initiative rather subtly from the university itself. In addition to being a clearing-house for information, it will suggest what it feels are appropriate directions for higher education. We are assured that suggestions for policy change in higher education from this agency will be no *more* than suggestions, and I believe these assurances. But even suggestions from such a source will have great power and obvious pressure elements, and they will encourage even greater participation by state government in academic decision-making than we have experienced hitherto. Governors and legislators are far more the key figures in the Compact of the States than are representatives of public higher education, numerically or in any other way.

A great deal of this has happened and will continue to happen because we are traditionally laggard in our efforts toward establishing and maintaining a systematic planning process within our institutions. When we ourselves do not make assessments and evaluations and judgments and extrapolations for the future, when we ourselves do not take the time to examine our society and its needs and to determine where such needs impinge upon our own responsibilities, we can only expect that others will seize the initiative from us. Indeed, I have heard governmental officials say, as a paraphrase of the old saw about generals, that the educational future is too important to be left in the hands of educators. If this is so, we have only ourselves to blame when we abdicate from any part of the responsibility for taking the initiative.

What I have been describing makes evident that this is not a simple problem to resolve. It also makes it clear that we should do well to re-examine our willingness to put all our faith and trust in the fact that our own particular situation may for the present be one of enjoying excellent mutual understanding and an uncomplicated partnership with state government. Some of us may think a sudden reversal of attitude is not probable or even possible. There is at least a reasonable likelihood, however, that we may be deluding ourselves.

The Need for Formal Guarantees

We have come to a time in the life of public higher education, I believe, when we should look carefully to the more formal, more legal safeguards to the independence of universities as our ultimate guarantee. Private institutions have such guarantees today by their very nature and much to their advantage. Furthermore, it is not mere coincidence that the very strongest of our state universities have their independence protected by clauses in their state constitutions. Autonomy may not assure academic excellence, but it most certainly is a major factor in providing the freedom of action that can lead more swiftly and surely to such excellence.

With the tendency of the times toward more and more interest in public higher education by the people and their duly elected and appointed representatives, and a corresponding tendency to introduce political considerations into the process of educational planning; with the growth in size of our institutions of learning, and their changing characteristics as a result of this growth requiring of them an ability and a freedom to make the most sweeping changes in every aspect of university life; with the enormous outlay of public funds for higher education, now and in the future, and therefore the mounting sense of vested interest by the public and governments; with more activist and vocal students and faculty on campus after campus calling attention to the academic world and causing increasing curiosity about what universities truly do and what they are supposed to be doing; with increasing pressures from business, industry, social agencies, or federal and state governments to shape the activities and curricula of the universities to their needs in research, training, and education and to give such needs the very highest priority; with the increase in abrasive challenges and charges inevitably hurled by both sides in any disagreements over the missions of universities—with all these factors and others, constitutional guarantees of university independence of action appear not only desirable but essential.

The precise nature of these constitutional guarantees is bound to vary from state to state, as experience has already shown us. The clauses we read in the constitutions of Michigan, California, and Minnesota, for example, differ considerably. Yet they all tend to achieve the same goal; in so doing, they have brought enormous academic strength to their state universities. They are illustrative of a principle we should not ignore, namely, that legal safeguards to independence contribute to academic excellence.

We are prone to fall into the common error of believing that growth in size must carry with it more rigid controls and regulations and less flexibility of opportunity. Professor M. M. Chambers states this so well when he says, "Whether we think of institutions or of persons, the greatest mistake we can make is to believe that because we are becoming more numerous, we must inevitably lose some of our freedom. *The opposite is true.*"[1] The task for large institutions now becomes one of being organized in such a way physically and academically within the necessities of being large that even greater academic opportunities present themselves.

It should be pointed out also that having constitutional guarantees of freedom does not necessarily mean taking advantage immediately, or indeed at any time, of all the possibilities these guarantees provide. For example, if a university finds that its relations with a state purchasing agency or budget agency are such that it is having done for it efficiently, economically, and without interference all it requires, that university need not make any change in these regards. But it is important for all to know that if at some future time interference begins to be evident, the university has the constitutional power to make a change. It should have something to fall back on for its protection from any external actions that show signs of making inroads upon its essential freedom. Only in this way can it move forward with complete confidence.

It is in every way unthinkable that public universities of our country, founded in permanent and time-tested traditions of freedom going back for eight centuries, given the mission of producing graduates who will be informed rather than indoctrinated and who will be capable of rendering independent judgments, given the equally dominant mission of exploring the unknown with indefatigable zeal and without limitation—it is unthinkable, I say, that these public universities should be subject to the temporal vagaries which political relationships are bound to stimulate. It is equally unthinkable that universities should not recognize their inevitable involvement with political figures and governmental agencies, and that they should approach such involvement with anything but the highest sense of responsibility and the utmost candor in communication.

The process of orienting external agencies to a fuller knowledge of university affairs is one never to be abandoned or weakened in any way; it is, in fact, a most necessary facet of university development. But all such orientation must be founded upon certain permanent strengths provided legally and guaranteeing the opportunity for universities to achieve greatness through independence and freedom of action in areas which are clearly reserved to them alone. Otherwise, we shall be allowing and even encouraging the fluctuations of fortune which personalities and events can bring about from time to time.

This, then, is the essence of my comments: that the public universities of today and tomorrow should have their basic freedom of action guaranteed to them by constitutional authority; that they should use their power under such authority only when necessary as a protection; and that they should deal responsibly, perceptively, and realistically with all elements of state government, seeking thereby to create a climate of understanding and trust which will make recourse to legal defenses unnecessary in all but the most extraordinary circumstances.

---

[1]M. M. Chambers, *Freedom and Repression in Higher Education* (Bloomington, Indiana: Bloomcraft Press, 1965), p. 120.

**See Section I in the back of this book
for annotated bibliography of related materials.**

Precis

Maintaining Institutional Identity and Autonomy in Coordinated Systems

Institutional autonomy is a relative concept. It is affected not only by external constraints but also by the attitudes and experience of those within the institution who are concerned about the state of its autonomy, be they students, faculty, staff, administrators, regents, alumni, etc. Briefly stated, the identity of an institution is the image established by the idiosyncrasies and dynamics of these constituents. The freedom they may exercise in establishing this identity determines its autonomy.

In California, external constraint, having an impact upon campus identity and autonomy, is produced by the interaction of the university system with the development of the Master Plan for Higher Education and the Coordinating Council for Higher Education. Other constraints upon the university system are generated by accrediting agencies, professional societies, and a variety of local, state, and federal agencies. Within the university system, the sources of influence are the regents, the offices of the president and vice-presidents, and university-wide committees.

Within the institution itself, the views held by faculty, staff, and students are of major importance in the development and maintenance of institutional identity and autonomy.

Faculty views reveal generally an initial tendency to equate institutional autonomy with personal autonomy. Autonomy is freedom from constraints except those deemed necessary and proper.

The initial comments of staff are not related to autonomy but to accountability. As an institution in a publicly-supported system of higher education, the campus is viewed as a public trust requiring accountability to all whom it serves or is served by.

The responses of students are of an entirely different character from those of the faculty and staff. The students are vitally concerned about the ends, or the results, which freedom of action presumably provides.

The maintenance of institutional identity and autonomy is no longer the responsibility of the administration alone, trying desperately to preserve the myth that the university is a sanctum for a collection of unencumbered free intellectuals. Students, faculty, and staff are the primary resources for achieving and preserving institutional identity and autonomy.

16

Chapter 2

Maintaining Institutional Identity and Autonomy in Coordinated Systems

by
Daniel G. Aldrich, Jr.
Chancellor
University of California at Irvine

N o thoughtful reading or discussion about the nature and function of a university will produce information supporting the view that these agencies of higher education are truly autonomous. Whether it be an individual entity or a member of a system, coordinated or otherwise, a university is a product of society and is subject to a variety of constraints, according to the particular forces which established it and the environment in which it functions.

Institutional Autonomy: A Relative Concept

Institutional autonomy, therefore, is a relative concept. It is affected not only by external constraints but also by the attitudes and experience of those within the institution who are concerned about the state of its autonomy, be they students, faculty, staff, administrators, regents, alumni, etc. Briefly stated, the identity of an institution is the image established by the idiosyncrasies and dynamics of these constituents. The freedom they may exercise in establishing this identity determines its autonomy.

In response to the invitation to discuss institutional identity and autonomy in coordinated systems and, hopefully, to add to the pool of information from which concepts can be developed concerning the organization and operation of a university, I shall identify, first, conditions and relationships in the system which are likely to affect the institution's freedom in establishing its identity. Consideration will be given to the stipulations and characteristics of the system, which, according to the goals and objectives of the institution, may be considered support for, or constraints to, institutional autonomy.

Recognizing that autonomy is a condition which may differ in character, depending upon the constituents within the institution making the judgment, faculty, administration, and student views of institutional identity and autonomy will then be discussed. With this information as background, a concluding effort will be made to identify and define those conditions or relationships within the enterprise which assure its autonomy and identity, regardless of the constituent making the appraisal.

In general, I shall be discussing the freedom and constraints experienced by faculty, administration, and students in developing and operating one campus in a nine-campus system in which ultimate authority and responsibility for the system rest in a Board of Regents. Specifically, I shall draw from my experience in planning, developing, and operating the Irvine campus of the University of California, which I have had the opportunity to serve as chief administrative officer since its inception.

In the university system of which the Irvine campus is a part, there are a number of organizational entities whose goals and responsibilities have significant impact upon the operation of the campus. In addition, there are organizations external to the system which affect its function. Some of the responsibilities and activities of these agencies within, and external to, the system will be described, so that fuller appreciation may be had of the reservoir of forces that act to influence the identity and autonomy of the institution.

From Without: Impact of the Master Plan

The Master Plan for Higher Education in California seeks to assure appropriate educational opportunities to all qualified students at reasonable costs to the people of the state and to guarantee essential expansion, without wasteful duplication, through the coordination of the three public sectors of higher education—junior colleges, state colleges, and the state-wide university system. The University of California, as a participant in the development of the master plan, continues to meet its traditional obligations for university-level instruction and professional training, research, and public service. According to the provisions of the Donahoe Act of 1960, by which the state legislature of California implemented the Master Plan for Higher Education in California, the University of California (1) adopted admission standards in 1962 under which the top 12½ percent of California high school graduates are eligible for admission, (2) embarked upon a program of adjusting enrollments by 1970 to a 60/40 ratio of upper division and graduate students to lower division students, (3) agreed not to introduce lower division instruction at new campuses until surrounding communities have developed junior college facilities to an adequate level, (4) improved its utilization of classrooms and laboratories to approach standards set forth by the master plan, and (5) developed a "Plan of Growth" which would enable the university to increase its present enrollment of approximately 80,-000 students to 120,000 by 1975 and 215,000 by the year 2000.

While fulfilling these requirements of the master plan, which have a pronounced influence on institutional identity and autonomy, the university also has been a conscientious and productive participant in the affairs of the Coordinating Council for Higher Education. This is an advisory body to the boards of the public institutions of higher education, established by the Master Plan for Higher Education in California, which (1) reviews the annual budgets and capital outlay requests of the University of California and state college systems and presents to the governor comments on the general level of support sought; (2) interprets functional differentiation among the junior college, state college, and university systems; and (3) develops plans for orderly growth and the need for, and location of, new facilities.

In addition to the impact upon campus identity and autonomy which is produced by the interaction of the university system with other segments of higher education in California, constraints are generated external to the institution and the system by accrediting organizations and professional societies and a variety of local, state, and federal agencies.

Within the university system, institutional identity and autonomy are influenced by the Board of Regents' policy, by policies and procedures, rules and regulations developed by the offices of the president and the vice-presidents, by numerous university-wide committees of faculty, staff, and students that deal with curricular and extracurricular, business and personnel affairs, and by the students, faculty, and staff of the institution itself.

From Within: Impact of Personal Viewpoints

With minor exceptions, no particular effort has been made in the foregoing commentary to characterize the effects of the system on the identity and autonomy of the institution as constraints or as opportunities. Such classification is dependent upon the goals and objectives of the institution and the constituency within the institution making the appraisal, whether they are faculty members, administrators, or students. Assuming that goals and objectives can be defined, I should like now to discuss the views these constituents hold on the development and maintenance of institutional identity and autonomy.

The Faculty: Search for Personal Freedom

An examination of faculty views reveals generally an initial tendency to equate institutional autonomy with personal autonomy. There is a desire to be free of all possible constraints in research, writing, teaching, and service, except those which might be imposed by whatever small group of professional or academic validators faculty members deem necessary and proper to pay attention to. Autonomy is freedom from "busy work" which intrudes upon research time, freedom to teach as though there were no other courses and no "red tape," and freedom to express social and political views, uninhibited by responsibilities of university citizenship.

Responses to specific inquiry concerning views about institutional autonomy within the university system depended on roles of the faculty, perceptions of the institution and system they share or do not share, and value-attitudes which might shape their responses to the environment. The obvious implication is that faculties generally do not exhibit homogeneous reactions to organizational factors.

Perhaps the prime factor in determining the reactivity of the faculty to the question of institutional autonomy is the level of confidence they have in the administration. When confidence is firm, the faculty who do not have administrative responsibility

20

develop the following spectrum of reactions to the idea of greater autonomy or decentralization of authority in the system:

1. Campus autonomy will not matter much, one way or the other.
2. "Red tape" (many forms and many copies) can, or will be, reduced.
3. Decentralization will mean home rule on important policy matters.
4. Opportunity for educational innovation will be enhanced.

Among faculty who administer (deans, department chairmen, etc.), greater freedom from capricious veto on personnel recommendations is expected, as is greater control over budget and greater freedom to experiment.

A certain ambivalence is evident in the faculty comments about institutional autonomy, for remarks concerning the desirability of greater freedom are accompanied by expressions of appreciation for the prestige and the political and moral strength attached to the university system as a whole.

Finally, those who see predominantly "good" in a centralized prestigious system are suspect of increasing autonomy, especially in the uncertain days of a campus's early development.

The Administrative Staff: Accountability, Not Autonomy

Turning from the faculty to views of administrative staff who are concerned primarily with the operation and fiscal affairs of the institution, the initial comments were related not to autonomy, but to accountability. As an institution in a publicly supported system of higher education, the campus is viewed as a public trust requiring accountability to all whom it serves or is served by. This is a fundamental constraint which the campus inherits as a member of this system. Since it is demonstrable that virtually every activity on a campus has academic implications, the public and its representatives must have a genuine understanding of the operation and mission of the institution and its need for freedom. To reduce the likelihood of outside interference, these institutions must avoid any practice which may give rise to the suspicion that management and fiscal affairs will not bear critical scrutiny.

In reviewing the activities of the Office of Business Affairs, which encompasses every dimension of campus life, it was possible to draw a number of conclusions concerning the involvement of the campus in the university system which would ensure maximum freedom of operation. These are:

1. There should be a continuing effort to place authority for decision at the campus level.
2. The development of uniform policies and formulas as controlling devices in the system should be minimized.
3. Excessive concern should be avoided about duplication of effort and the centralizing of "housekeeping" activities which may interfere with efficient local management.
4. There is a stifling effect of system on institutional initiative and creativity. Autonomy is not the province of a single agency; it is the concern of many sub-units of the agency, as well as of those external to it.

The Students: A Means to Ends

The responses of students to queries about institutional autonomy were of an entirely different character from those of faculty and administrative staff. Little concern was voiced about the means or the machinery for achieving and maintaining autonomy. Instead, the students were vitally concerned about the ends, or the results, which freedom of action would presumably provide. They were preoccupied with the idea that they have opportunity "to leave their mark on the campus." They wanted access to the administration and sought assurance that the institution would afford them the opportunity to be involved in making decisions which would influence the character of the campus. While there was interest that their campus be free of pressures from other campuses of the university system in the planning and development of student organizations, programs, and activities, great appreciation and admiration were expressed for the excellent reputation which the system, as a whole, has achieved and for the opportunity to be identified with it. There was a genuine hope expressed that their institution would afford them the opportunity to excel, so that they might participate responsibly and productively in the university system's continuing quest for excellence. In short, the students were far more concerned about identity than they were about autonomy. But, buried in their comments, was the assumption that somehow and in some way they would be free to drive toward their goals.

Out of my discussion with faculty, students, and administrative staff, concerning institutional identity and autonomy, has come a number of ideas and concepts about the organization and operation of a university, which should obtain, if the climate of freedom in which higher education flourishes is to prevail.

Institutional Identity: A Must for Autonomy

In some ways, institutional identity is a prerequisite to institutional autonomy, for only as goals and objectives are defined can the constituents of the institution determine whether the conditions of the system in which they operate are constraints or opportunities. As circumstances permit better definition of the opportunities and constraints in the system, its members may well experience greater autonomy. They are able to enlarge the scope of their independence in constructive ways, for by invention they can push back the boundaries of constraint.

The more the individual understands the goals and objectives of the institution and his role within it, the more likely he is to accept stipulations and changes in it as conditions which may ultimately ensure him the freedom he desires. Willingness to accept constraints as a condition of achievement will be found more often when the goals and objectives of the individual or the institution are similar to those of the system.

From the point of view of higher education, the foregoing observations indicate that a new kind of organization is in the making, at least insofar as faculty involvement is concerned. No longer is it possible—if it ever was— for the faculty member to think of himself as a free agent, unencumbered by operational requirements and administrative constraints. The price of faculty freedom today is an increasing amount of faculty time spent in becoming knowledgeable about the goals, objectives, and operation of their institution and the particular role that they play in it. The faculty member will have to become more of an organizational man, since the resources he requires to support his teaching and research programs have to be generated from much more complex systems. He cannot shun involvement in the operation and administration of the institution. Faculty participation and leadership will be indispensable in the conduct of the institution's affairs and in the development of resources to support it.

Increasingly, faculty will have to take the initiative in obtaining outside validation for their needs and, in doing so, will be assuming greater responsibility for generating leadership within the institution.

The maintenance of institutional identity and autonomy is no longer the responsibility of the administration alone, trying desperately to preserve the myth that the university is a sanctum for a collection of unencumbered free intellectuals. Today the preservation of conditions which will encourage, rather than limit, intellectual freedom and institutional independence involves every individual in the institution. Knowledgeable about, and dedicated to, the goals and objectives of the institution, aware of their roles and their responsibility for developing leaders and providing leadership, prepared and expected to assist in the acquisition of adequate material support and in the development of public appreciation of the values of higher education, students, faculty, and staff are the primary resources for achieving and preserving institutional identity and autonomy.

**See Section II in the back of this book
for annotated bibliography of related materials.**

Precis

Politics and Current Patterns in Coordinating Higher Education

One of the most influential factors leading to the strengthening of the states' role in higher education is the coordinating agency which acts in liaison between both the state and national capitols and the higher education institutions.

The fifty states continue to experiment with three different types of coordinating systems: The voluntary council, consisting of public college and university presidents and board members; the single governing-coordinating board for all state supported institutions of higher education; and a board super-imposed over the governing boards of individual institutions or systems. The trend is toward the third mentioned board composed of citizens who do not directly administer or govern any public institution.

The general movement toward creation of coordinating boards of citizen members with substantial powers has been accelerated by three trends now better understood and better identified than previously. Simply stated they are:

1. The coordinating agencies are exercising more and more political leadership in formulating and advocating policies for development and expansion of higher education.

2. More and more federal grant programs for higher education are being state oriented rather than institution oriented.

3. The non-public colleges and universities are becoming more involved in public policy-making and coordination for all colleges and universities.

The confidence of the public and of college administrators, governors, and legislators may be a fickle asset when an agency finds itself in a political crisis, whether from errors in judgment or honest attempts to achieve objectives unacceptable to those with greater power. Yet, the long-range interests of higher education must be promoted through political leadership whatever the attendant risks to the coordinating agency or to the persons engaged in the role.

Chapter 3

Politics and Current Patterns in Coordinating Higher Education

by
Lyman A. Glenny
Executive Director
Illinois Board of Higher Education

Today, higher education institutions cooperate more closely with each other and with government than at any previous time in American history.

Probably the most significant advances in cooperation and coordination are coming about through ties created by the state and national capitols. Over the years, the state capitol provided more initiative and exercised more control in promoting higher education than the national government. Although that condition appears to be subject to radical change in the near future, the results are unlikely to make national education dominant. Several factors, such as increased awareness by the states of their responsibilities, the new philosophy of creative federalism, and the activities of state governors and other officers in improving state administration, make that outcome less imminent than some educational and political leaders believe.

The State Coordinating Agency

One of the most influential factors leading to the strengthening of the states' role in higher education is the coordinating agency which acts in liaison between both the state and national capitols and the higher education institutions.

Coordinating agencies for public higher education have been so generally adopted by the states that a historical discussion seems out of place. Ten years ago knowledge about them was little and understanding of their functions even less. Now, the great majority of states maintain some agency which attempts to make more rational the complexities of college and university development. Both collegiate administrators and governmental authorities have accommodated themselves to this nascent agency which promises to gain increasing significance as it matures. Logan Wilson, president of the American Council on Education, provides in a recent paper the reasons why coordination is here to stay:

> Our past assumption has been that the separated aims and activities of existing colleges and universities would somehow add up to the best educational interests of the nation. In my judgment, this is no longer a valid assumption. Higher education has become too complicated, too costly, and too important in the national welfare for its basic decisions to be made haphazardly.[1]

To achieve Mr. Wilson's "best educational interests," the fifty states continue to experiment with three different types of coordinating systems. First, serving fewer and fewer states, is the voluntary council consisting of public college and university presidents and board members; secondly, maintained by a static number of states, is the single governing-coordinating board for all state supported institutions of higher education; and finally, an increasing number of states have super-imposed a coordinating board over the governing boards of individual institutions or systems of colleges and universities. The latter agency commonly referred to as "The Higher Board" (or some similar appellation) varies widely in its composition and powers.

The trend is for coordinating boards to be composed either of a majority or a totality of citizen members who do not directly administer or govern any public institution. State legislatures and governors have delegated increasing power to such boards over state-wide planning, budgets, educational and research programs, and other matters pertaining to the expansion of the total state higher educational complex. Thus, the trend toward a majority of public members seemingly encourages an increase in power. Conversely, the policy-making branches of state government show reluctance to extend significant power to boards composed primarily of institutional presidents and governing board members.

The Trends Toward Coordination

The general movement toward creation of coordinating boards of citizen members with substantial powers has been accelerated by three other trends now better identified and better understood than previously.[2]

Simply stated they are:

1. The coordinating agencies are exercising more and more political leadership in formulating and advocating policies for development and expansion of higher education.
2. More and more federal grant programs for higher education are being state-oriented rather than institution-oriented.
3. The non-public colleges and universities are becoming more and more involved in public policy-making and coordination for all colleges and universities.

Each tendency, in mutual re-enforcement, promises to continue indefinitely. The order of listing the trends indicates their priority of importance, and although the future often makes fools of social scientists who predict historical events, in my opinion these trends portend significant consequences to patterns of coordination and cooperation in higher education. The reasons are revealed as we examine each of them in some detail.

The Political Leadership Role of Coordinating Agencies

While both collegiate administrators and state government policy makers find acceptable most coordinating agency activities, their conception of the political role of the agency remains unclear. Yet that role may now be the most important of all those played by coordinating agencies since it makes possible a new and different kind of positive leadership. Russell Cooper in a recent book on college administration states:

> Unfortunately, the kind of amateurish leadership that sufficed reasonably well fifty years ago is not adequate for modern institutions, with their multimillion-dollar budgets, their hundreds of fiercely independent faculty members, and their critical place in American society.[3]

A Scheme of Balanced Tensions

The coordinating process is a political one, involving powerful social agencies, such as colleges and universities, with their historic intellectual independence and autonomy on the one side, and the central public policy-formulating authorities of the governor and legislature on the other.

The coordinating agency, situated between these two powerful political forces, seeks to identify with both in order to achieve satisfactory solutions to developmental and financing problems of higher education. The agency role may appear to be strictly one of arbitration or of mediation, but it extends much further. Today, its principal legal duty is long-range planning for improving educational quality and for expanding programs and facilities. The responsible exercise of that power necessarily takes from both the universities and the state authorities a valued traditional function; this, in turn, provides the coordinating agency the means to political leadership.

The necessity for state-wide planning is now generally accepted by all concerned, and, recognizing their own limitations, legislatures assign to coordinating agencies the task of recommending public policy for higher education. Ultimately, however, legislators must act on agency recommendations. While they are relieved not to have the responsibility for determining priorities among contending colleges and universities for additional funds and facilities, at the same time they may be resentful of the agency's objective planning proficiency which discourages purely political decisions in such matters as location of new campuses and allocation of funds to institutions.

The coordinating agency's policy strength is built on expert fact-finding and extensive studies by technicians and leading citizens. In a sense, recommendations by the coordinating board, in the public interest, bar legislators from achieving parochial interests. Of course, recommended policy must be approved by a legislative majority and if a sufficient number of powerful legislators should block recommendations, the coordinating board could lose the proposal and simultaneously become vulnerable to outright abolishment or circumscription of its power.

In accepting the need for state-wide planning, university administrators and governing board members are not as apt as legislators to place confidence in a coordinating agency, and in fact often oppose its establishment. Nevertheless, once authorized and operating, a spirit of cooperation generally prevails between institutions and the new agency. However, collegiate administrators sometimes resent long-range plans recommended to the governor and legislature by the agency, for the same reasons as do some legislators. The limited outlook of a university, in creating new branch campuses or professional schools or of trying to obtain more than an equitable share of state funds, may be contrary to effective master plan developments of higher education.

Thus, if recommended coordinating policy runs contrary to aspirations of a sufficient number of powerful university administrators, the coordinating board may find itself subject to open attacks in public forums and *sub rosa* by the governor and in the legislature. Its power could be reduced or eliminated if the seeds of destruction land on fertile soil.

Legislator and university administrator alike sincerely believe they promote the public welfare in pursuing their particular interests. As John Gardner has stated in his book on *Excellence,* "They may well recognize their leadership role with respect to their own special segment of the community, but be unaware of their responsibility to the larger community."[4] If in practice, this unawareness is manifest in the pleadings of individual legislators or administrators, their objectives will be looked upon by peers and the public as "special interest" unworthy of adoption as against proposals of a coordinating agency which ostensibly has given thorough study to all state-wide interests in arriving at recommendations. (This is not to say that coordinating agencies never misjudge the public interest.)

The increase in political influence of the coordinating board results directly from the support of the governor, legislators, and college administrators, the great majority of whom work for the broad public interest. Hence, the forces which could destroy the coordinating agency by direct and indirect attack actually have given it the support and confidence necessary for success. This situation is a paradox when one considers that the coordinating agency has no built-in constituency, no tradition, little public awareness of its purpose and function, and operates on monies appropriated by the legislature. Yet, the coordinating agency must face tensions generated by universities and colleges through extensive constituent arousal means, such as alumni associations, grand openings of new campuses, dedication of new buildings, free tickets to influential public officials for sporting events, dinners, and concerts, and a public relations staff dedicated year-around to molding a citizenry favorable to institutional aspirations. On the other side, too, tensions arise from legislative and executive branches whose local and state-wide political constituencies are organized for support and who have access to the effective communications media for reaching the public.

Thus, tension is the key to the new leadership. Tensions among elements in the coordination scheme do not entirely dissipate even in smoothly operating systems and, fortunately, can not. Indeed, the process is similar to the workings of a democratic society and may be described as a "system of balanced tensions" among diverse elements.

Exercises of Powers

State-wide, long-range planning is the principal legal power which allows the coordinating agency to gain a degree of political leadership in the "scheme of balanced tensions." Priorities and determination of need for new programs, new buildings, and new campuses logically follow from a grand design which is subject to continuous reassessment and revision in order to reflect the dynamics of societal change. As master planning becomes a continuous process, the agency gains insight and sophistication in higher education policy-making and its consequences.

Within the prescribed policy perimeters of a master plan, the agency may properly exercise its short-run functions of budgeting and program approval without the capricious characteristic of expedient *ad hoc* planning. The more clearly defined the long-range objectives, the more rationally and easily made are decisions on immediate expansion plans of individual institutions or systems of institutions. Such planning also works to the advantage of the collegiate administrators and state officials in that both have a basis beyond aspiration and wishful thinking for making decisions.

Subordinate to, but part of, agency planning power is budget review. This power, too, is exercised with far more sophistication than previously. System-wide studies of unit costs and of building capacity and utilization often produce valuable information. In greater use today are formulas and sub-formulas which reflect the differences among institutions in types of programs, level of students, and unit costs. Positive efforts to prevent "uniformity" and "leveling" are now more characteristic of some coordinating boards than, say, of some universities maintaining branch campuses under a central administration.

For implementation of master plans, several additional powers recently have been delegated to the agencies. Some of the most common are establishing minimum admission standards, approving non-academic construction projects, setting minimum tuition and fees, and discontinuing programs.

Compromise vs. Public Interest

The success and longevity of the coordinating agency are largely determined by its attitude toward maintaining high-level dialogue and the "system of balanced tensions." Two different modes of coordination now prevail among the thirty-eight to forty states which have one of the three types of agencies previously mentioned. Both modes result less from powers granted or assumed by the agency than from its composition. They stem from the conception of leadership held by the board or council and its staff. The modes are not as clearly delineated in practice as they are described here, although agencies can be identified which closely approach one mode or the other.

Coordinating Agency as a Broker

One mode is that of the coordinating agency which looks upon itself only as a mediator or arbitrator among the conflicting forces at work on higher education, and thereby assumes the role of a broker in the political market. This role of balancing power and accommodating interests in higher education has been carefully described by Clark Kerr as it relates to the position of president in a multi-versity.[5] The chief strength of this method is the resulting policy which avoids the frustrating of powerful interests and thus avoids outright opposition. Many group interests may be partially satisfied in order to achieve harmony, but no influential group is completely disaffected.

The deleterious outcome of market-place policy-making is succinctly stated in a recent publication on American politics entitled *The Consent of the Governed* by Professors Livingston and Thompson. The authors state:

> Present political realities tend to reflect a situation in which public policies express only bargains hammered out on the anvil of compromise . . . and they enable us to respond with half measures, at best, to pressing public problems.[6]

Three interrelated weaknesses can be associated with the brokerage role.

First, the role forsakes initiative in leadership, especially in state-wide planning and in meeting changes effectively. Proposals from institutions overlook many state-wide conditions and generally reflect an egocentric attitude, placing the particular institution at the center of developments. Such proposals frequently do not depart from traditional practices or policies of the individual colleges. The coordinating agency in the broker role may then have available only compromises which result in "half measures" rather than a viable state-wide policy promoting the total interests of higher education. Philip Selznick, a noted scholar on large-scale organization, wrote disparagingly of this avoidance of leadership:

> In particular, if a leadership acts as if it had no creative role in the formulation of ends, when in fact the situation demands such a role, it will fail, leaving a history of uncontrolled, opportunistic adaptation behind it.[7]

Second, the brokerage approach encourages only the strongest forces to seek rapprochement while ignoring those too weak politically to be a threat. The result is dominance by one or more of the most powerful institutions, generally the leading state university, and possible continuance of conditions which the coordinating agency was created to rectify. As Victor Thompson has written of this type of coordination:

> What appears to be a frank, open, rational, group problem-solving process is very often actually a bargaining or political process. The outcome is likely to be determined by power, even though on the surface it seems to be a result of rational analysis.[8]

Third, since dominant institutions try to maintain their position and their autonomy, a safe approach to all major change becomes the prevailing attitude. The leaders in effect say:

> Unless we, the center of learning and the leading university, undertake this function (new campus, building program, or study) it will not be done well, and it is likely to threaten the very integrity of this outstanding center of excellence.

Status quo becomes the order of the day.

The brokerage method thus underplays any leadership role for the coordinating board, a condition, incidentally, looked upon with great favor by the dominant universities. Needless to say, some existing coordinating agencies, either for lack of vigor or to save their lives, use the compromise method almost exclusively. It is, of course, more prevalent in voluntary organizations but has acceptance in some legally established agencies as well. Such agencies pose little or no direct threat to the aspirations or autonomy of any institution, but their passive role may well fail to protect the weaker institutions from the strong and in a real sense abrogate their responsibility to the public.

Victor Thompson summarizes the brokerage method of coordination as follows:

> Coordination through group identification is coordination based upon the common conscience, upon similarities of psychic content, and cannot, consequently, extend far enough to include all activities which need to be coordinated. The interdependencies arising from specialization extend much further than the face-to-face working group. The reliance upon group solidarity, therefore, is regressive—one might say a measure of desperation. It should be noted, furthermore, that to the extent that group identifications cannot be perfectly manipulated, their promotion involves some loss of control and is therefore self-defeating from the standpoint of the promoters.[9]

The process is self-defeating and discredits the agency charged with coordination. On great issues of higher educational expansion and development, the stakes of the leading institutions are of such importance that compromise becomes intolerable. Rather, the theme becomes "every man for himself" and its corollary *lex talionis*. Because of acquiescence in the brokerage method, the coordinating agency lacks the will, knowledge, and leadership essential for advancing the public interest in times of crisis. When this point is reached, only the governor and legislature, the last resort in harmonizing all state policy, have power and prestige enough to settle such disputes. Failure by a formal coordinating agency to recommend a sound policy promoting the best interests of higher education encourages the legislature to reconstitute the agency and revitalize its powers.

Coordinating Agency as Leader

The other mode of coordination, increasingly sought by governors and legislatures, is one which provides leadership in planning for all major aspects of higher education development. Such agencies are not expected to be mere mediators among the universities. They are expected to assert the kind of positive leadership that James A. Perkins recently espoused for university presidents.[10]

This second mode of operation, as previously asserted, depends heavily upon the composition of the board or council. Those agencies with a clear majority of citizen members not directly connected with the governance or administration of public colleges or universities tend to exercise vigorously the new leadership role anticipated by the legislature and governor. The attitudes of such citizen boards usually contrast substantially with those agencies inclined to the brokerage mode.

The effective citizen agency looks upon the entire province of higher education as its responsibility. It gains knowledge and detailed facts and figures throughout the state about all post-secondary school institutions, small or large, public or non-public, junior college or advanced graduate. It strives for universal high quality while opening opportunities for all potential students, rich or poor. It seeks equity for each institution whether politically weak or strong. It aims at positive goals in the orderly development of the state's collegiate system and exercises negative controls only when infringement on master plan objectives or the rights of other institutions impend.

Further, in its plan of operation, administrators and other experts, drawn from all types of colleges and universities, civic organizations, business, and government, become involved in agency study and policy-making procedures. These people provide technical knowledge for solution of immediate and long-range problems. More important perhaps, they become the principal means of intercommunication between the general public and the state coordinating structure.

Through such widespread citizen participation in formulation of policy, the agency may itself create an influential constituency. Contacts, which this constituency has with other local and state organizations and their leaders, foster exchanges of knowledge, views and argument which are reflected ultimately in coordinating policy. Faculty members, too, enter the dialogue as important independent spokesmen for higher education. Unlike many college administrators, faculty members generally commit their professional expertness without strong bias toward the more parochial aspirations and objectives of their institutions.

Policy developed in this manner, in contrast with the brokerage method, first considers the broad public interest while directly involving the leadership of colleges and universities whose destinies are at stake. The parties most likely to be disaffected in this process are presidents and board members of the largest state universities who, because of their own power, look with more favor upon the confrontation and compromise method so characteristic of their voluntary coordinating councils.

Implications for Institutional Autonomy

We find throughout the United States an increase in power for the coordinating agencies. Some powers granted were formerly exercised by the legislature, others by the governing boards of institutions, and still others, such as state-wide planning, are new in concept. Theoretically, subordination of colleges and universities to a coordinating board is an impairment of institutional autonomy. But the degree of that impairment must be viewed in comparison to the actual, not the theoretical, autonomy which formerly existed. Impairments by the legislature and the governor were not unknown and some limitations on freedom of action certainly resulted from the unlimited political and financial competition of institutions with each other, particularly in legislative halls.

Again, the relative merits and benefits to be gained from living in a lawfully ordered society must be considered as against the freedom of unregulated competition. The real issue is over the degree to which coordination infringes on institutional freedom essential to the advancement of knowledge, the exploration of ideas, and the critical assessment of society itself.

College and university administrators sometimes propose that higher education should be a self-governing fourth branch of government entirely independent of legislative and executive controls. Others take a less extreme view but express alarm at the kinds of powers now exercised by the state either directly by state executive and legislative arms or indirectly by a coordinating agency.

Too often, however, the self-government advocates have a proclivity to press for freedom only for their own institutions, especially for material goals such as additional funds or additional campuses. If life among educational institutions has not been "nasty, brutish, and short" as Hobbes stated in another context, it has been highly competitive, with the strong gaining the lion's share, and the weak the lamb's. As Ivan Hinderaker recently stated, "All men are not inherently evil, but in any competitive situation there are likely to be some who will stoop to whatever will get by."[11]

Voluntary coordination among state-supported institutions has succeeded only for short periods of time because the leading state university could be magnanimous without threat to its dominant position. However, once weak colleges gain in strength, they ungratefully descend upon their benevolent big brother, thus ending voluntary coordination. This creates conditions necessitating formal coordination and regulation.

A second difficulty with this conception of autonomy is the lack of differentiation between that which is substantive and that which is procedural. Modern society, with its multitude of laws, regulations, and controls, provides in a positive way for more diversity and freedom of choice and action than at any previous time in history. Freedom without law is far more restrictive than freedom within societal law. By asserting certain controls and rules in the interest of orderly, rational, and equitable development, all the colleges and universities in the state system stand to benefit. The procedural rules established and the practices engaged in by coordinating agencies seldom touch upon the day-to-day decisions or affect adversely the substantive educational and research functions of an institution.

Those leaders of universities which are the most powerful financially and politically may resent even procedural impediments in their path to "manifest destiny." Leaders of smaller institutions aspiring to create by replication "The" prestigious state university resent controls which curb that possibility. Coordinating agencies become unpopular with some institutions when they terminate the oligopoly type of competition which is called "unfair" in the business world, even though these "cease and desist" coordinating practices also tend to remove higher education from the partisan and pressure-group politics of the state.

Initial popularity, however, is not as true a test of whether co-ordinating agencies interfere unduly with valued autonomy as is the prevailing attitude of college and university administrators after the agency has been in operation for several legislative sessions. Seldom, if ever, have university administrators attempted to abolish a formal coordinating agency. They have little desire to return to unpredictable legislative lobbying and pressure tactics, whatever nostalgia may arise for such activities when attempting to gain a dramatic expansion unlikely to be provided in a state-wide master plan.

Master Plans: Effectiveness of Non-Educators

This discussion, which may seem to some unduly cynical or perhaps extreme, points up the reasons why the new type of co-ordinating agency, devoted to master plan implementation in the public interest, is proving more successful in the legislative halls and executive offices than are other coordinating structures or modes of operation. The techniques of involving many prominent citizens, outstanding college and university administrators, and experts from all walks of life, result in plans for legislative action which carry a receptiveness unlikely to be associated with plans developed out of negotiated compromises. In addition, the legislature is less likely to attack or amend the real substance of such a plan, whereas plans based upon a bundle of compromises invite legislators to renegotiate the agreements.

Federal Programs and Implications for Coordination

The second great trend toward more cooperation and coordination in higher education finds its matrix in the national capitol rather than that of the state. Federal grant programs not only encourage new activities; they also tend to strengthen coordination at the state level.

One of the new axioms of state administration is that if you wish to give permanence to an agency, assign to it administration of a federal program. If the axiom proves true, some coordinating agencies now have built-in longevity. They also seem to have acquired new means for drawing non-public institutions more closely into coordinating studies and plans.

Title I of the Higher Education Facilities Act of 1963 provides grants to colleges and universities for construction of academic facilities. For administration at the state level, it requires an "agency which is broadly representative of the public and of institutions of higher education." Generally, the governor designated the existing coordinating agency if it was constituted of public members as well as representatives of institutions. If not, citizens were added to membership or a new agency was created to meet this requirement.

Subsequently, the Higher Education Act of 1965 made the same "broadly representative" requirement in the administration of Titles I, IV, and VI. These provide grants, respectively, for community services and continuing education, scholarships and loans, and for certain instructional equipment. The U. S. Office of Education requested the governors to appoint, if possible, the same agency for the new Title VI as for the 1963 Facilities Act. Only a few governors have failed to comply. In most cases, in states where the board was properly constituted, Titles I and IV of the 1965 Act were also assigned to the existing coordinating agency.

Throughout the country, these titles and others, such as the Vocational-Technical Education Act and the Technical Services Act, are now administered by a variety of state agencies, and only a minority of states have as many as three or four of them centered in the legally constituted coordinating board. Nevertheless, the eventual designation of the coordinating board to supervise most of the programs, which are clearly higher educational and which require an agency broadly representative of the public and the colleges, seems almost a certainty. This will be especially true if the agency membership and mode of operation concentrate on, and actively reflect, the public interest.

The Three Pressures for Synthesis

Three developing conditions provide support to the idea of placing federal programs under a coordinating agency.

First, the number of federal programs and the diversity of state agencies administering them will eventually require coordination. Some federal acts already call for close coordination with previously authorized federal programs and for auditing and validation of data from colleges and universities. All collegiate institutions are accustomed to working with a plethora of agencies, private, federal, and state, yet few agencies have asked to audit books and accounts or to make on-campus checks of data as required by the new federal acts. Institutions themselves will demand a consolidation of such activities in order to limit the number of different on-campus reviews and of the number of agencies with which to deal.

Second, the states and particularly the governors, who designate the state agencies for administration of federal programs, are finding that many have considerable potential for overlap with each other and with those of state origin. Consequently, federal requirements to coordinate may well be matched by state demands for similar action. The more dispersed the administration of these programs, the greater will be the demand for consolidation, especially as each expands in scope and funding. Some governors have already anticipated coordinative needs by designating one or two agencies to administer most of the new programs, and the state coordinating board usually has received the major assignments.

Third, and most important, state governments will become aware that federal programs administered through several different agencies do not efficiently support implementation of a state master plan for higher education. In fact, the agencies, even if not working at cross purposes to the plan, will usually have independent goals in mind. As conflicts occur among goals, state coordinating boards will request the governor to reassign or coordinate federal activities in a manner to produce maximum attainment of master plan objectives. Several boards have already suggested this policy to governors and have received sympathetic responses.

Evidence indicates all three of these tendencies toward greater coordination are gaining momentum at this moment.

Concern in Non-Coordinated Areas

A consequence not yet mentioned is that states without legally established coordinating agencies now have boards or commissions to administer one or more federal programs relating to colleges and universities. In some states these agencies, not initially constituted for state-wide coordinative purposes, have been given additional higher educational tasks to perform for the state. As centralization of federal programs and state assignments come about, the agency may in practice take the form of a regularly established coordinating board. This back-door approach may be used by governors in states where it has been difficult to obtain the full benefits of formal coordination. If one considers that such agencies must, under federal law, be composed of members representing both the public and colleges, the agencies have the potential of becoming a "public interest" coordinating board.

These trends have already caused concern, if not alarm, among certain university administrators and their national associations. The land-grant colleges and universities have traditionally dealt directly with the federal government. This practice provides a great deal of independence from state legislative and executive control and the recent attempt of the President to reduce certain "land-grant" funds in favor of the new grant programs administered through the state understandably aroused the concern of these university administrators. So much so that Congress restored the funds in the appropriations bill. Similarly, the American Council on Education, which has been generally favorable to state planning and coordination, now appears to be opposed to further strengthening the state's role with federal funds.

The philosophy of "creative federalism" as expressed by the President and other spokesmen for the national government, may be even more frustrating to collegiate administrators. The new attitude is for fewer federal "strings" to be attached to money awarded the states and for fewer programs to be administered directly from Washington. Administration of Title I of the Higher Education Act of 1965 is an excellent example of allowing the state to determine what problems will be attacked and what means will be used in finding solutions. With continued and mounting pressures from virtually all major state sources for more federal funds and fewer restrictions on their expenditure, "creative federalism" will gain support despite the efforts of the Land-Grant Association and the American Council on Education to obtain more federal funds granted directly to the universities, thus by-passing any state agency.

Coordination and the Non-Public Colleges and Universities

As a result of state-wide master planning and of federal grant legislation which applies to non-public as well as public colleges

42

and universities, non-public institutions are being drawn into the coordination process at an accelerated rate. Thus, the capitol and the non-public campuses achieve closer and closer relationships.

Constitutional Barriers to Including Non-Public Schools

The constitutions of most states (Pennsylvania, Maryland, and New York being noteworthy exceptions) prevent any controls or financial aids, direct or indirect, for non-public colleges, particularly those with a church affiliation. This historical situation has not changed substantially in recent years, but neither has it barred state surveys and master plans from increasingly involving the non-public institutions with the public on a voluntary and co-operative basis. They have become an integral participant in studies of students, faculties, programs, and facilities and sometimes indirectly gain from the final plans.

One substantial gain has been provision for tuition scholarships which may be used either in public or non-public colleges. States with these popular scholarship programs periodically increase the total money available as well as maximum amounts awarded individual students. It is not unusual for two-thirds or more of the total funds to go to students attending non-public colleges. Such scholarship programs, of course, have no restrictive state controls incident upon institutions.

Non-public colleges also benefit from other master plan actions. Plans for expansion of programs and campuses of the public system of colleges consider as fully as possible the contributions already being made by non-public institutions. Sites of new public junior colleges and senior institutions are selected with an eye to protecting non-public colleges, particularly if such colleges are not highly restrictive because of tuition costs, admission standards, or church affiliation. Non-public professional schools (medical, dental, engineering, and architectural), invariably become integral units in the analyses of need to expand programs in public institutions.

Federal Non-Differentiation Between Schools

In addition to the indirect aids provided the non-public colleges, some federal programs now require that no differentiation be made between public and non-public institutions in approving grant applications. With this partnership in federal programs, the

43

state agencies involved have as much contact with many non-public institutions as with those in the public system. Despite the federal intent to treat all institutions alike regardless of who controls them, state agencies are in a position, through selection and weighing of priority criteria, to favor almost any type or size of institution. For example, by such activity on the part of the co-ordinating agency in one state, two-thirds of the funds available for senior institutions under the Higher Education Facilities Act have been awarded to non-public institutions. Other states, of course, have heavily weighed the criteria most helpful to the public, or to the small, or to the large institutions as the case may be. The more sophisticated the state administrators of federal programs, the more they are able to serve by indirect means certain groups of institutions as against others.

The Drawbacks to Private Institutions

The serving of institutions with federal dollars also has its drawbacks. The experience with administration of the Higher Education Facilities Act across the country indicates need to make on-campus checks and audits of data which are used to establish project priorities among the applicants. Some states already make such checks and others, on the verge of doing so, will no doubt include them at the time the state agencies verify institutional data and conduct financial audits as required under Title I of the Higher Education Act of 1965.

Without a doubt, these verification procedures will be resented by administrators of non-public colleges in the states where relationships between the state and the colleges have been remote. Even public college administrators who endure many audits may not look with favor on still more. Nevertheless, it is axiomatic in the American democratic system that tax funds must be expended only for the purposes designated by the appropriating body. To ascertain such compliance, verifications and audits are essential. To reassert a point made previously, it would seem probable that in order to limit the number of different state agencies having such intimate relationships with institutions, those in the non-public segment, as well as the public, will be seeking centralization of the federal grant programs in a single state agency, probably the state coordinating board for higher education.

As a result of state master plan involvement and the federal grant programs, many leaders of non-public colleges and universities have already developed cooperative and friendly relationships with the staffs of coordinating agencies.

Just as the coordinating board stands in liaison between the public college and the state, so too, does it increasingly serve this function for the non-public institution in relation to both the state and the public colleges. And in this social process another force with political power is added to the coordinative system of balanced tensions.

Coordination: Its Promises and Risks

The purpose of this paper has been to describe recent trends in state coordination of higher education. Particular emphasis was placed on the political leadership role of coordinating agencies and on the influence of federal grant programs in strengthening that role with respect to both public and non-public colleges and universities. The paper sought to describe a model coordinating agency in composition, power, and mode of operation, knowing the while that models are seldom produced in fact and that even the best of real agencies sincerely devoted to the indefinable "public interest" may at times poorly plan, overplan, or commit blunders in political leadership. The author is fully aware that confidence of the public and of college administrators, governors, and legislators may be a fickle asset when an agency finds itself in a political crisis, whether from errors in judgment or honest attempts to achieve objectives unacceptable to those with greater power. Yet, the long-range interests of higher education must be promoted through political leadership whatever the attendant risks to the coordinating agency or to the persons engaged in the role.

Lastly, the author is under no illusion that coordination provides a final panacea for higher education any more than higher education is the panacea for all ills of the society, but both have promise and evidence of achieving certain highly desirable goals if positive and imaginative leadership is asserted.

[1]From his paper presented at 20th National Conference on Higher Education, Association of Higher Education, March 1965, Chicago, Illinois.

[2]See T. R. McConnell, *A General Pattern for American Public Higher Education,* New York, McGraw-Hill Book Co., 1962, and also Lyman A. Glenny, "State Systems and Plans for Higher Education," *Emerging Patterns in American Higher Education,* Wilson Logan (ed.), Washington, D. C., American Council on Education, 1965.

[3]Russell M. Cooper, "Improving College Teaching and Administration," *Higher Education, Some New Developments,* Samuel Baskin (ed), New York,, McGraw-Hill Book Co., 1965, p. 213.

[4]John Gardner, *Excellence,* New York, Harper and Row, 1961, p. 125.

[5]*The Uses of the University,* Cambridge, Mass., Harvard University Press, 1963.

[6]The MacMillan Co., New York, 1966, p. 32.

[7]Philip Selznick, *Leadership in Administration,* Evanston, Illinois, Row, Peterson & Co., 1957, p. 75.

[8]Victor A. Thompson, *Modern Organization,* New York, Alfred A. Knopf, 1961, p. 189.

[9]*Op cit.,* p. 186.

[10]"The New Conditions of Autonomy," American Council on Education *op. cit.,* p. 8 ff.

[11]"Ethics in America, Norms and Deviations," *The Annals of the American Academy of Political and Social Science,* Jan. 1966, p. 28.

See Section III in the back of this book
for annotated bibliography of related materials.

Precis

The Federal Government and Higher Education: Old Answers Breed New Questions

It seems almost inevitable that eventually the nation must consider federal support for the totality of higher education—support for the system as a system. In spite of the fact that achievements may be left to the next generation, we should begin debating possible approaches. There are four basic propositions to be understood before an understanding and an evaluation of future federal roles in higher education are reached:

1. The nation needs an increasing supply of college graduates in all fields; we can afford no loss of potential talent. We are, perhaps, facing the need less realistically than our forebears a century ago faced up to the need for universal elementary and secondary education.

2. Our existing structure of higher education is strong and diversified, representing a sizeable investment, but parts of the system are under severe financial strain.

3. Recent U.S. Congresses and national administrations have demonstrated a conviction that the federal government has a major role to play in financing higher education.

4. In spite of, or perhaps because of, this infusion of federal funds, the fiscal situation of many of our institutions is more precarious than it was a decade ago. This is so, in part, because the demands on our institutions are increasing more rapidly than available resources, but also because federal support has been almost entirely categorical and requires the commitment of additional institutional funds.

If limited institutional funds are to be spent in vital areas, in addition to those categories now partially supported by federal funds, then major readjustments in funding formulas—and in concepts of the responsibility of higher education—are going to have to be made. Included in the areas of necessary exploration are: facilities, housing and academic; graduate education; research; student aid; development of major university centers; undergraduate centers; and institutional cooperation and division of labor.

Somewhere answers are going to have to be found to the new questions raised by present methods of federal support to higher education. Who is going to do it? The hour is at hand when higher education must say, "These are the things that must be done, and these are the ways we must do them." If we fail to come up with our own answers, we shall have no one but ourselves to blame if we don't like the answers that are provided us.

Chapter 4

The Federal Government and Higher Education: Old Answers Breed New Questions

by
John F. Morse
Director, Commission on Federal Relations
American Council on Education

If I may, this morning I should like to share with you a series of propositions and questions that increasingly preoccupy me as I sit at the hinge-point of the government-university world. Most of the things I want to talk about are, I think, your direct concerns. The answers we as a nation eventually come up with—or our failure to come up with answers (and this seems to me inconceivable)—will profoundly affect your work. Let me start with four basic propositions.

Basic Propositions Leading to Questions

1. The nation needs an increasing supply of college graduates in all fields. We can afford no loss of potential talent. Such statements may seem to point the obvious, but as a nation we have not truly come to grips with the financial implications a commitment to their fulfillment will entail. We are, perhaps, facing the need less realistically than our forebears a century ago faced up to the need for universal elementary and secondary education.

2. Our existing structure of higher education represents a sizeable investment and a major national resource. Much has been written of the strength of our diversified system. Yet parts of that system are under severe financial strain.

49

3. The last five congresses and the last three national administrations have demonstrated a conviction that the federal government has a major role to play in financing higher education. Through the programs of executive departments and agencies and a series of legislative enactments, important support has been provided for many of the functions of higher education in its triple role of research, teaching, and public service.

4. In spite of, or perhaps because of, this infusion of federal funds, the fiscal situation of many of our institutions is more precarious than it was a decade ago. This is so, in part, because the demands on our institutions are increasing more rapidly than are available resources. It is also true because federal support has been almost entirely categorical, and because almost every federal program requires the commitment of additional institutional funds.

The American Council on Education has consistently supported the concept of categorical aid to higher education. It continues to do so. We have stated a series of priorities and at the top of the list has been, and continues to be, the provision of facilities—housing and academic—to meet the inevitable increase in enrollments. Second only to the need for facilities has been the need for adequate student aid programs to bring higher education within the reach of qualified but needy students. An encouraging but inadequate start has been made toward meeting both these needs.

It is clear, however, that if higher education is to meet its own commitments and commitments being made in its name by the federal government, something beyond categorical aid will be required. Ways must be found to provide general institutional support, not as a substitute for but as a supplement to categorical support. It is essential that organized education as an entity and, equally important, the federal government *as an entity* review existing programs and develop a rationale for the host of relationships that characterize the government-university partnership. Higher education can perhaps live indefinitely with, and adjust to, the requirements of an individual government program or of a whole executive department, even if those requirements tend to warp institutional purpose or constitute a drain on institutional resources. But as federal programs proliferate in number and grow in size, their total impact has severe consequences for all institutions.

The Use of Institutional Funds for Federal Projects

We have noted above that one characteristic of most existing federal programs is that they require the commitment of additional institutional funds. A few examples will serve to bring home the point.

1. Because of congressional insistence on institutional cost-sharing, government-supported university-based research will require this year the commitment of approximately $60 million in institutional funds.

2. By the end of this year over $100 million of institutional funds will be invested in the National Defense Student Loan Program. Institutions will also be absorbing approximately $6 million annually in administrative and collection costs.

3. The level of construction anticipated this year in the Academic Facilities Program will require the commitment of at least $1¼ billion in non-federal funds.

There is a certain logic in all of this. It can be argued that the federal government is merely providing assistance for the universities to do what they would in any case be bound to do. A further argument is that matching requirements tend to stimulate the flow of non-federal dollars. But there are fallacies in the argument as well.

1. Institutions would not, because they could not, undertake, on their own, programs of the size and scope now being supported with federal funds.

2. Ability to provide matching funds or to share costs varies greatly. The more impoverished institutions are therefore increasingly less able to participate.

3. Most federal programs engender a need for continued and increased investment of institutional funds.

A single program, small in scope, may illustrate all of these points. A program entitled *Upward Bound* is being supported by the Office of Economic Opportunity. Its purpose is to identify promising students at the tenth and eleventh grade in high school who, because of long years of deprivation, will be clearly unable to qualify for higher education. Through intensive summer remedial programs and week-end instruction during the academic year, institutions hope to be able to bring these students to their potential grade levels and prepare them for higher education. The legislation governing this program requires that institutions contribute out of their own funds 10 percent of the cost of operating the program. In addition, O.E.O. has arbitrarily imposed a limitation of payment of no more than 20 percent of indirect costs, regardless of actual and audited indirect costs. The result is that in a typical approved project entailing an expenditure of $183,000 O.E.O. will provide $152,000 and the university must provide $31,000.

The official position of the director of O.E.O. is stated as follows: "My personal view is that cost-sharing in Upward Bound denotes the partnership that exists between this agency and the colleges in meeting an educational need which has been ignored too long." With the limited perspective of one agency director considering one program this is a reasonable statement. But if one were to extrapolate that $183,000 to $3.6 billion (roughly the level of all federal support at the present time) and the institutional share proportionately to roughly $620 million, the fallacy becomes obvious.

Furthermore, if Upward Bound, which is still experimental, is successful, we will be moving into the colleges large numbers of additional students who will need teachers, academic facilities, housing, and large sums for financial aid to fulfill our commitments to them—all to be provided under cost-sharing requirements. As institutions dedicated to public service we must, of course, hope for success, but success under current federal policies will create new problems.

To date, the strains on institutional budgets have been met in two ways which must be continued and in two ways which cannot much longer be tolerated. State appropriations and private philanthropy have been stimulated as the critical importance of higher education has increasingly won recognition. This trend must continue, and federal policies must be so shaped as to encourage it. Budget deficits and charges levied on students have increased sharply. This trend must be reversed and federal policies must be so shaped as to prevent their necessity. We believe that in the years ahead every existing federal program should be examined, and new programs should be designed with these concepts serving as guidelines. The following specific areas require attention, and in giving them attention we must find answers to some hard questions.

Facilities: Should the Student be Billed

Historically, academic and housing facilities have been provided to institutions outright, through state appropriations and through philanthropy. Thus, in the past, it was necessary to charge students (if at all) only an amount sufficient to cover operation and maintenance. When, however, it became necessary, beginning in the 1950's, to construct in one or two decades more plant than had been built in the previous three centuries, a new pattern of financing emerged. Loans for college housing which, theoretically at least, can be self-liquidating have led to the necessity of charging room rents which would cover debt service as well. Construction of academic facilities through grants covering only a small proportion of construction costs and through loans is leading to a similar situation in which the institution must increase its fees to cover operation, maintenance, and debt service.

1. Would a sharp increase in the federal share in grants for academic facilities construction assist in stabilizing student fees? What should that share be?

2. Would legislation which supported new construction to replace obsolete facilities lead to greater efficiency and hence lower costs?

3. Are loans, except in exceptional circumstances, viable instruments for providing new academic facilities? For providing housing? If so, can loan programs be so revised as to make the debt service less burdensome on institutions and, in the final analysis, on their students?

Graduate Education: Healthy Colleges and Anemic Universities

Historically, graduate education has been concentrated in private institutions with large endowments and in public institutions in our wealthier states. The nation's need for manpower educated beyond the baccalaureate level was small in proportion to the total population or even the undergraduate population. Beginning in the 1950's, however, the need for such manpower in all fields, but particularly in college teaching, became explosive. Federal policies now encourage institutions with limited resources available to them to move in to meet this need.

1. Is current federal support of graduate education sufficient to meet a reasonable share of the cost of that education?

2. Put another way, is the desire of more and more institutions to move toward more advanced degrees in more fields, and the encouragement by the federal government for them to do so, changing healthy colleges into anemic universities?

3. What percent of institutional resources previously assigned to undergraduate education is being drained off by the expansion of graduate education? How is graduate education affecting both the quality and the pricing of undergraduate education?

4. If graduate education, more than any other level of education, is a national, rather than a regional, state, or local concern, would it be appropriate for federal funding to be concentrated at this level? This would call for providing larger sums for institutional costs, library facilities and collections, and academic and research facilities.

Research: Always an Education Process

Most, but by no means all, research supported by the federal government in universities is inextricably interwoven with and essential to graduate instruction. Most of it, too, is essential to the fulfillment of the missions of the governmental agencies providing the support. Current government-wide policies require that universities share in the cost of supporting this research "at more than a token level." Although it can be argued that, because of a mutuality of interest, cost-sharing is logical, the net effect of the policy is to drain institutional resources or—to put it another way—increase the cost of graduate education. Furthermore, to the extent that the research does not significantly support the education process, it constitutes a drain on instructional dollars.

Other areas of concern in the realm of research include the government's almost total reliance on the project system and its understandable determination to concentrate research in institutions of demonstrated excellence. Few could argue that project support should be reduced or that funds should be diverted from our great centers of learning. Yet ways must be found to permit more institutional determination of what research and researchers are to be supported. Furthermore, ways must be found to provide to institutions of lesser renown, which must continue to educate the vast majority of students, opportunities to work on the frontiers of knowledge and to grow in distinction.

1. Has the time come when cost-sharing in governmentally-supported research should be the exception rather than the norm? Might it even be sound national policy to provide funds over and above the full cost of such research as a means of strengthening the total program of the institutions?

2. Should all research-supporting agencies develop programs of institutional grants as supplements to project grants for the support of basic research? On what base and through what kinds of formulas can such programs be developed?

3. Can ways be found to involve more institutions in the government's research effort without a sacrifice of quality and without weakening our strongest institutions?

Related Functions: For Whose Benefit?

Since World War II the government has, with increasing frequency, turned to higher education for expanded and often entirely new services. Some of these services are directly related to the main functions of higher education; others are at best peripheral. A partial list would include: the education (and the training) of increasing numbers of foreign students; major programs of technical assistance to the developing nations; expanded programs in extension, adult, and sub-professional training; major attacks on new and unresolved urban problems; the training of workers for a variety of new federal programs such as the Peace Corps, Vista, and the like; the establishment, staffing, and management of Job Corps camps; development of new or expanded programs in such fields as oceanography and water and air pollution. All of these programs require the commitment of university manpower resources and, ordinarily, their financial resources as well. The time has come for a sober assessment of the ability of higher education to carry out the many roles society is asking it to undertake.

1. Is it possible to define the concerns of society to which higher education is uniquely qualified to address itself?

2. Has the time come, and will society accept the concept, for higher education to reject certain tasks now thrust upon it? Should some of these tasks be channeled to profit and others to non-profit enterprises or be performed, in-house, by government?

3. Can there be a reconsideration of the impact on the manpower and financial resources of higher education, of the increase in national problems to which higher education is being asked to address itself?

Student Aid: Borrowing by Students, Not by Parents

The answer to many of the above questions will determine future patterns of student financial aid, for their resolution will inevitably affect pricing of education. The government is increasingly committing itself to the full support of postbaccalaureate students on the premise that highly skilled manpower is the nation's most critical need. Its policy, or lack of one, in the support of undergraduate students is more confused. In general, however, the drift is toward encouraging heavy borrowing by students to pay for undergraduate education. Existing legislation will result in $6-10 billion in student borrowing in the next five years. This is resulting in our transferring the responsibility for meeting college costs, intentionally or unintentionally, from the parental to the student generation.

1. What are the effects of such a shift likely to be? Will it seriously affect patterns in seemingly unrelated areas such as career planning, marriage, real estate, and consumer products?

2. Would governmental programs designed to keep costs (and therefore pricing) down result in greater economies than allowing pricing to spiral and providing more massive programs of student aid to bring higher education within the reach of all? Or should we continue our current pattern, which is placing pricing closer to costs, and bridge the gap with bigger and new programs of student aid?

3. Should our ultimate national goal be the provision of free education at all levels? Would the return in future tax income from anticipated higher earnings balance the initial outlay that such a policy would require?

The Creation of Major University Centers

Some believe it clearly the intent of the government to increase the number and the geographical distribution of major university centers. Others see the drive in this direction as reflecting the intent of certain influential legislators and institutions rather than as a clearly defined congressional or administration policy. In any case, current policies designed to develop new centers are confused. Certain programs of the U.S. Office of Education, the National Science Foundation, the National Aeronautics and Space Administration, and less overtly of the Department of Defense, the Public Health Service—National Institutes of Health, and the Atomic Energy Commission are addressed to this problem. Obviously, an ill-defined, uncoordinated, multi-agency drive is not the best way to achieve such a goal.

1. How can the higher education community assist in the identification and then the development of new major university centers?

2. Is it desirable, and are there ways, to coordinate and focus the programs of many governmental agencies on agreed-upon ends in agreed-upon centers?

The Cost of Undergraduate Institutions

There is general agreement that the flow of federal funds to major universities is having a deleterious effect on primarily undergraduate institutions. This concern is related only in part to the flow of *research* dollars.

1. Can and should the government address itself to the problems of these undergraduate institutions? Can programs be devised to help them retain first-rate faculty? to assist first-rate faculty to retain their "first-rateness"?

2. Can existing federal programs be retailored, or new ones devised, that will enable these institutions to attract, and warrant attracting, first-rate students?

Institutional Cooperation and Division of Labor

As government needs, particularly in the field of research and graduate education, become more costly, rational determination rather than *ad hoc* decisions will increasingly be required.

1. Will large and complex centers under the direction of a single institution be the pattern? Or are we likely to move increasingly toward the consortium-managed centers?

2. What will be the division of labor among institutions? Who will determine it?

3. Should basic decisions rest in the states? or groupings of states? In this context, what are "the states"? At the present time there are individual institutions, associations of institutions (public and private), state commissions created as a result of federal legislation, chief state school officers, and governors, all contending to be thought of as "the states" and all to some degree supported in this contention by some federal program. Is this a healthy manifestation of diversity? Or is it confusion approaching chaos?

University Cooperation: A Transfer of Power

Increasing attention must be given to the structure of the executive and legislative branches of government in their relationship to higher education. But equally important, institutions must devote attention to their own structure for dealing with government. The increasing number and complexity of government programs will almost force a decentralization of decision-making, program management, and fiscal oversight away from Washington, D.C. and to individual institutions. Most institutions are ill-equipped at the moment to handle such a transfer.

1. How can government procedures be simplified and made more uniform to facilitate such a transfer?

2. How can institutions be assisted to reorganize to accept such a transfer in a way that will assure proper stewardship of public funds and the fulfillment of public purposes?

Broader Areas to be Explored

In the discussion above an attempt has been made to identify a few specific segments of higher education that require attention.

If we can find satisfactory answers to the questions posed, we shall have moved a long way toward some major solutions.

Nevertheless, the sum of the parts so far discussed does not add up to the whole. It seems almost inevitable that eventually the nation must consider federal support for the totality of higher education—support for the system *as a system*. How this is to be achieved must, perhaps, be left to the next generation. Even now, however, we should be debating possible approaches. The following suggest the kinds of questions that might be asked:

1. Should there be further revisions in tax laws to encourage increased contributions to higher education from individuals and from corporations? What should they be, and can they be so devised as to prevent erosion of the tax base?

2. Is a possible approach the one currently being discussed—that of returning to the states a portion of the federal tax? Under such a scheme how could we preserve the balance between public and private (sectarian and non-sectarian) institutions?

3. Would a government-wide policy of full reimbursement for all federally supported categorical aid programs free sufficient non-federal funds to provide adequate support for institutional programs? If not, would a "payment for service" surcharge provide a solution?

4. Would it be desirable for the government to expand greatly and extend broadly the "endowment of instruction" concept of the Morril-Nelson Act? Would it be desirable and possible to extend this concept to private institutions? to church-related institutions?

5. Might an alternative approach be the payment of a federal "cost-of-education" subsidy to the institution in which each student enrolls? What controls would be necessary in order to prevent expansion-at-any-price becoming the prevailing policy at some institutions?

I ask you to forgive what must have sounded like the reading of a laundry list. I am fully conscious of the fact that not one of the major areas I have touched on has been adequately treated. Each one alone could be the subject of a talk longer than this one. If the series of questions I have asked was exhausting, let me assure you it was not exhaustive. Let me close by saying that these questions are going to be answered by someone—somehow. They are going to have to be. But who is going to do it?

This is an age of White House conferences. It is an age of anonymous Presidential task forces. It is an age of government planners and computer programing. A couple of years ago when some one said that education is too important to be left to educators, it was considered a wisecrack. Today I see signs of its becoming doctrine. I suggest that the hour is at hand when higher education must say, "These are the things that must be done, and these are the ways we must do them." If we fail to come up with our own answers, we shall have no one but ourselves to blame if we don't like the answers that are provided us.

*

**See Section IV in the back of this book
for annotated bibliography of related materials.**

Precis

The Effects of Federal Support on the Allocation of Campus Resources

Not only are federal disbursements in line with a long-standing American technological tradition, but they are also highly concentrated in other ways. As late as fiscal 1964, 85 percent of federal funds for higher education were disbursed for organized research. In fiscal 1962, 95 percent of federal research funds in educational institutions were devoted to work in the physical and life sciences.

Federal disbursements are highly concentrated geographically. In 1961-62, seven "rich" states received 66 percent of federal payments. They accounted for 43 percent of degree credit enrollment. Thirteen "poor" states received 7 percent of the federal contribution; they enrolled 14 percent of the nation's students. Federal money is also distributed in ways that allow large numbers of graduate students to devote full time developing research skills.

There is more to be said for the present system than against it. However there are some trouble spots. What are possible sources of inefficiency in American higher education? Some might be: inadequacy in quality of faculty; teaching or learning the wrong things; devaluing the education of under-graduates; and the plight of the poorer states and of their gifted students.

In asking whether federal involvement has helped cure the inadequacies in quality of teaching, the answer is clearly positive. One cannot be so positive in speaking of the effects of federal aid upon other sources of inefficiency.

One solution might be to provide the states with block grants to use in strengthening all higher education within their boundaries. The states, though, would still be responsible for accounting to the government for the manner in which the funds were spent and evaluating the success of those programs advanced with federal funds.

In World War II the government had the most urgent need for scientific research, and it naturally turned to the strongest institutions to get it. From the point of view of the development of higher education in the U.S., has necessity now become virtue? There are problems to be solved. Our society is rich enough to afford an even more complete search for talent.

Chapter 5

The Effects of Federal Support on Allocation of Campus Resources

by
Charles S. Benson
Associate Professor
of Education
University of California
Berkeley, California

The Concentration of Federal Funds

The first observation I would make about federal involvement in campus affairs is that our central government has rather consistently followed a policy of building on strength. As late as fiscal 1964, so the Office of Education reports, 85 percent of federal funds for higher education were disbursed for organized research.[1] In fiscal 1962, 95 percent of federal research funds in educational institutions were devoted to work in the physical and life sciences.[2] Ever since the time of Benjamin Franklin, our country has been regarded as one that valued a rather peculiar combination of pure and applied research in scientific fields: pure research is fine if a certain amount of it is sure to lead to practical applications; applied research is all right, too, as long as a certain amount of it does more to better the human condition than add to the profits of manufacturers.

Not only are federal disbursements in line with a long-standing American technological tradition, but they are also highly concentrated. In 1961-62, the following states received 66 percent of federal payments toward the current fund income of institutions of higher education: California, Illinois, Maryland, Massachusetts, Michigan, New York, and Pennsylvania.[3] (I refer to "total" federal

63

disbursements, not just to payments in support of organized research.) Each of these seven states is known to have at least one major, nationally regarded institution of higher education, or an institution that can be described as a "university" in the highest sense. Each of the seven is in the top quarter of states with regard to personal income per capita, which is to say that all of the seven are rich. Among them they accounted for 43 percent of degree credit enrollment, obviously a smaller proportion than their share of grants represents. In contrast, thirteen poor states, Alabama, Arkansas, Florida, Georgia, Kentucky, Maine, Mississippi, North Carolina, North Dakota, South Carolina, South Dakota, Tennessee, and West Virginia, had 14 percent of the nation's enrollment and received 7 percent of the federal contribution toward current fund income. Federal programs, including those in lower education, ordinarily provide more dollars proportionately in the poor states than the rich. Federal participation in higher education is an exception.

Not only is federal money concentrated both with respect to subject fields and geographically; it is distributed in ways that allow large numbers of graduate students to devote their full energies to developing their research skills. This period of full-time research training ordinarily occurs in the life of the student when he is in his early twenties, that time, apparently, when he is most likely to have great amounts of energy to acquire these kinds of new capacities. What I refer to, of course, is the project system of grants and the support by the government of major research centers and national laboratories. Such subventions lead to the employment of large numbers of research assistants. It is perhaps interesting to note the contrast on this point between two institutions that are heavily involved in federal research grants and two that are not strongly involved. It is reported that, in 1962-63, there were 2,100 part-time positions in organized research at the University of California and 411 at Cornell. On the other hand, there were only ten at the University of Kentucky and fifty-two at the University of Maine.[4]

In World War II the government had the most urgent need for scientific research, and it naturally turned to the strongest institutions to get it. From the point of view of the development of higher education in the U.S., has necessity now become virtue? It is my feeling that there is more to be said for the present system than against it. However, I would like to suggest some trouble spots in due course.

Inadequacy in Quality of Faculty

Let us begin in rather general terms. What are some possible sources of inefficiency in American higher education? One might be inadequacy in quality of faculty. That is, under a social welfare function, the country as a whole might be "better off" if the colleges and universities of the land were staffed by people of greater abilities than is presently the case. I know of no way to express quantitatively the relation between quality of faculty and some kind of index of national welfare, but I am willing to assume that higher education occupies a strategic position in promoting national welfare and that improvement in calibre of faculty is thus an appropriate goal of national policy. Has federal subvention of higher education had favorable effects on this score? I think the answer is clearly positive. By concentrating funds by field and institution, the government made it practically certain that some faculty members would appear as Bunyan-like figures, men larger than life, men holding, indeed, the fate of their fellow creatures in their hands. Not only has status of the professional life been enhanced almost beyond measure, but so also have financial rewards been raised. This latter has happened more quickly (in terms of total earned income) in some fields (science, engineering, medicine, economics) than in others, but in academic life money does rub off. The creation of a moneyed elite in the university has benefited the pocketbooks of us all.

Teaching the Wrong Things

A second source of inefficiency would be for the faculty (as a group) to teach the wrong things and, similarly, for the students (as a group) to study the wrong things. I cannot see that federal aid to higher education has had much noticeable effect on these matters. In spite of the concentration of federal money in scientific and medical fields, we do not appear to be burdened with a surplus of scientists, engineers, or doctors. In Harold Orlans' book, *The Effects of Federal Programs on Higher Education*, the case is made that there has been little shift in the academic abilities of students who major in the sciences as compared with those who choose humanities.[5] What we may have been doing is simply exploiting the talents of the scientifically inclined more completely.

Further, I suspect that the federal grants have spilled over into the humanities, though I cannot give a quantitative estimate of the amount. Insofar as this has happened, and assuming that most young people do not have a completely open choice between, say, physics and literature, the humanistic faculties in the great universities have moved in a better position to attract the most promising students and help develop their abilities.

The argument about spill-over is commonly cast in the following terms. Assume that the receiving institution has a priority schedule of programs and projects for its next year's budget. Assume further that the institution faces budgetary constraint; that is, the institution on its own resources is unable to fund all the programs or projects it considers desirable. Suppose the programs (let us stick with just that designation) are listed x_1, x_2, x_3, . . . , and that the university decides it can support proposals for spending through x_n. Now, let the institution receive additional federal grants. It is likely that this money will support at least some of the x_1 to x_n spending proposals. Insofar as it does so, the university can then expand its next year's budget to include x_n+1, x_n+2, etc. Indeed, it has been suggested that the federal government should acquaint itself with these kinds of secondary effects of its grant programs.[6]

Under this sort of argument, it is at times when the rate of expansion in federal support of the sciences is slackening—or when, as now, the volume of federal research funds appears to be in absolute decline—that the humanities suffer most. To state otherwise is to assume that the universities stand in the same relationship to the federal government that a private, profit-making research organization does. That is, a relationship under which there is a precise dollar-for-dollar connection between the federal contribution and the amount of scientific activity supplied.

Devaluing Undergraduate Teaching

Education, however, can also be inefficient if the quality of instruction is inappropriate for the learning requirements of students or if the milieu of instruction is unaccepting of their condition. I feel these are serious problems at the undergraduate level and that the federal government is partly to blame. As I shall suggest later, it seems that appropriate corrective action can most properly be taken in the public sector.

It is a matter of common agreement that federal emphasis on research, particularly research in the "hard" subject fields, has served to devalue undergraduate teaching. What are the particular functions of undergraduate teaching? The successful lecturer will raise the motivations of the students in his audience. In what at Princeton are called preceptorials, the student engages the preceptor and his fellow students in discourse, partly for the fun of it and partly because the testing of ideas among peers sharpens one's capacity to think. The "section" provides a chance for the leader, commonly a TA, to help students over the rough spots in a course by patient, detailed explanations. For whom are these functions important? I suspect they are extremely important for the student from a non-college family. It is he who needs the stimulation of the outstanding lecturer; it is he who can most urgently use the self-confidence a good preceptorial can engender; it is he who can stand or fail on the help he gets from a section man.

I say these things apply on the average, and they apply because the non-college household will supply less intellectual nourishment than professional households. That is, the student from the non-college household has a smaller stock of intellectual resources, as distinct from talent, from which he can draw to become a self-sustaining member (in this case, student member) of the academic community. Worse, the students from non-college households typically attend poorer elementary and secondary schools than do children from professional families. It should be recognized that our institutions of higher education are superimposed on a system of lower education characterized by shocking inequalities of provision. Thus, when federal research expenditures abet the devaluing of undergraduate teaching, those who suffer are the same persons who have been poorly served in the ordinary public schools. Thus, there is a glaring inconsistency between the Elementary and Secondary Education Act of 1965, under which strenuous efforts are being made to improve the school opportunities for the children of the economically disadvantaged, and the generally-acknowledged implication about adverse effects of past federal higher education programs on undergraduate teaching.

It seems to me, finally, that the problem of undergraduate teaching is particularly acute in the great universities. This, after all, is where the government has concentrated its money. I feel that in such institutions the problem can be ameliorated, but not to the extent that it disappears as a problem.

There is also the matter of universities in the poorer states. Here, a few figures may be in order. Educational expenditures for students in 1961-62 varied from under $1,000 (Arizona, Oklahoma, Texas) to over $2,300 (Massachusetts, and excluding the usual "unusual" figure for Alaska), or by a factor of 2.3 to 1. Expenditures in instruction and departmental research had a smaller variation: the largest was about 1.6 times the smallest. The explanation, or at least a possible explanation, goes like this: large expenditures per student imply substantial amounts of federal money for research.

These monies are correlated with the existence of large graduate schools. The graduate schools supply teaching assistants to keep costs of undergraduate instruction in check. In 1962-63 at the University of California there was one part-time professional position for each 1.3 full-time persons and at Cornell, the number of part-time posts exceeded the full-time. At the University of Kentucky, on the other hand, there was one part-time person for each 8.7 full-time and at Maine, one part-time for each 4.8 full-time.

The great universities have developed a means to control undergraduate teaching costs and they also had, of course, large and varied financial resources before the period of federal intervention. Naturally enough, they pay high salaries for top-grade faculty, and they get a large share of the professional talent in the country. They also provide, in relatively handsome measure, auxiliary services. At the University of California in 1962-63 there was one professional librarian per 115 resident undergraduates; at Cornell the figure was one per 80 undergraduates. At the University of Kentucky it was one per 148 students and at the University of Maine, one per 396.

The Poorer States and Gifted Students

In Maine, the very bright mobile student will seek to go to a major university on the outside. But having lived in the state, I know that many students are too isolated economically, socially, and intellectually to attend an institution outside Maine. By the laws of probability this group contains some very bright students. But the institutions available to them are short of top-rated faculty,

68

deficient in auxiliary services, and bled of a due proportion of outstanding students (from whom other outstanding students ordinarily learn so much).

Now, it can be claimed that these two problems, the problem of the average-appearing, though possibly gifted undergraduate at the major university and the problem of the gifted but intellectually starved undergraduate in the isolated, poor state, are not really serious ones. I feel, however, that our society is rich enough to afford an even more complete search for talent and, secondly, that where the search is already rather broad-based, it is socially eroding for a person to make the effort to get in to college and then find that in spite of his efforts he does not "fit in." With respect to state universities like Maine, one might argue that the institution should not strive to be a university. Unless it is, however, it cannot serve the brightest students. Further, the research and cultural opportunities a university provides promote the economic growth of the area, which is a point commonly advanced in support of the efforts of underdeveloped countries to establish universities.[7]

More federal money in forms other than research expenditures would be a help, and, indeed, we are told that federal support, other than for research, was to rise from $1.9 billion in 1965 to $2.5 billion in 1966.[8] However, it is appropriate to recall Alice Rivlin's observations (*The Role of the Federal Government in Financing Higher Education*) that major federal aid for institutional support is inherently wasteful (the federal government is less able than the states to distinguish among institutions with respect to quality) and is likely to lead to conditions on block grants that are seriously damaging to institutional autonomy.[9]

One Solution: Block Grants

I think the answer to the problems I have raised here is federal money—but not earmarked federal aid to higher education. With the exception of Massachusetts, I am impressed that those very states that have well-financed state governments are at the same time the ones that have first-rate institutions of higher education. Thus, the important thing to do may be to use the revenue-raising power of the federal government to augment the financial resources of the state governments—through block grants, perhaps, under a Heller-type proposal.[10] In states that already have a strong university, the money—higher education's share of it—could be used to develop teaching institutions such as state colleges and junior colleges. In states that presently have a weak university system, the money could go for salaries, libraries, etc., in the university, but also for institutes, the type of expenditure that the legislative analyst in California refers to as "seed money" to build research strength and ultimately to attract federal grants.[11] Where the university in a state is necessarily small, it would seem appropriate to specialize in the research function, and the institute offers an appropriate means toward this end. It might also be appropriate to use some undergraduates as research assistants in the smaller universities.

Demands of the Government Auditor

As a last point, there is another type of inefficiency with which universities can be plagued: excessively detailed and sometimes spurious efforts to meet the demands of government auditors, all this to serve the end of public control of federal aid to higher education. I think we might all agree with Dean Price of Harvard that federal grants should be somewhat more broad-based than they generally are under the project system.[12] It is possible that the research and development centers established by the U.S. Office of Education could serve as a model in this regard. William Bowen of Princeton, in his comparative study of U.S. and British universities, reached the same conclusion, namely, that less restrictive types of grants would serve the cause of institutional autonomy in the American university.[13]

I would go further and also suggest that Dean Price is right when he holds that the federal civil service should have greater influence than it now does in making grants. My acquaintance with departmental officials and my reservations about the functioning of the committee system, at least in the field of education, lead me to this conclusion. However, as a corollary both to broader-based grants and to reliance on departmental judgments in making awards, it seems appropriate that universities move ahead with their efforts to establish better systems of program accounts. After the fact, it will still be necessary to show *in general* what the federal money has bought. Before the fact, program accounting helps to show departmental officials *in general* what the money is likely to buy and what the opportunity costs of the institutional resources are.

70

In conclusion, I would say that, though highly concentrated according to subject fields, particular states and economic regions, and to the advantage of graduate students, federal aid to higher education has been of tremendous benefit where it has been applied. It has played a major role particularly in strengthening faculties in those more fortunate states and institutions which have been primary recipients of aid.

There are gaps, nonetheless, in federal involvement in higher education, and I would question the failure of our universities and governing officials to identify the problems and apply solutions to them now. Federal aid has done little to convince faculty members and students alike to readjust themselves to teaching and learning more vital subjects than they now concentrate upon.

Federal aid has tended to devalue higher education at the undergraduate levels, thus compounding the inadequacies and inconsistencies already prevailing in our systems of elementary and secondary education. Government involvement has favored the already rich states over the poor states and further increased the disadvantages of students in those states, who for a variety of reasons must remain in their states to obtain a higher education.

These are a few of the areas untouched by the federal programs. They can be too easily dismissed as unimportant, but I think that we have the resources available now to get into them and to do something. One solution would be to give the states blocks of funds for higher education and let them put their experience and judgment to use in applying them fruitfully. That is one solution; there are others, and the time is here to find them.

[1]Office of Education, Preliminary Report of Financial Statistics of Institutions of Higher Education, Fiscal Year 1964, Based on a Sample of Institutions, Washington, Government Printing Office, July, 1964, p. 1.

[2]Special Sub-Committee on Education, Committee on Education and Labor, House of Representatives, *The Federal Government and Education*, Washington, Government Printing Office, 1963, p. 56.

[3]Office of Education, *Digest of Educational Statistics*, 1965 edition, Washington, Government Printing Office, 1965. pp. 98-99.

[4]These and other data about individual institutions are taken from Office of Education, *Statistics of Land-Grant Colleges and Universities, Year Ended June 30, 1963*, Washington, Government Printing Office, 1965, various tables.

[5]Harold Orlans, *The Effects of Federal Programs on Higher Education*, Washington, The Brookings Institution, 1962. p. 38 ff.

[6]H. W. Singer, "For Plans of Projects," *Economic Journal*, September, 1965.

[7]Frederick Harbison and Charles A. Myers, *Education, Manpower, and Economic Growth,* New York, McGraw-Hill Book Company, 1964, pp. 57-58.

[8]Committee on Labor and Public Welfare, U.S. Senate *Hearings on the Higher Education Act of 1965,* Washington, Government Printing Office, 1965, pp. 170-172.

[9]Alice M. Rivlin, *The Role of the Federal Government in Financing Higher Education,* Washington, The Brookings Institution, 1961, pp. 163-165.

[10]The proposal, commonly attributed to Walter W. Heller, professor of economics, University of Minnesota and formerly Chairman, Council of Economic Advisers, is that the federal government turn back to the states a share of the annual increase in its tax receipts, for the general use of the states.

[11]California Legislature, 1965 Regular Session, *Analysis of the Budget Bill of the State of California,* a Report of the Legislative Analyst to the Joint Legislative Budget Committee, Sacramento, California, Office of State Printing, 1965, pp. 321-322.

[12]Don K. Price, "Federal Money and University Research," *Science,* January 21, 1966, p. 288.

[13]William G. Bowen, *Economic Aspects of Education: Three Essays,* Princeton, Industrial Relations Section, 1964, p. 79 ff.

See Section V in the back of this book

for annotated bibliography of related materials.

Precis

The Compact for Education

The intention is to suggest that any discussion of the Compact for Education must be primarily a discussion of the future. The organization is formally in existence, but it is not yet really off the ground. What is the problem? Partly it is a matter of time and partly of expectations beyond the realm of likely results. The job now is to see that the organization does move, and in the right directions.

The story of the compact begins with James B. Conant's Shaping Educational Policy, published in 1964. He found education in a state of disarray. He traced much of the trouble to local control of the schools and to competition for state legislative appropriations among the public colleges and universities. Why not, he asked, work toward a nation-wide policy in this field? Regional agreements had been successful, why not try for more?

In the history of the formation of the compact, Terry Sanford is as important as Conant. The proposal as contained in Shaping Educational Policy is very general. Sanford gave it shape. He did so in remarkably short time.

Sanford naturally inclined toward an organization giving prominent position to governors; there was certainly good reason for this. By doing so he was able to move the compact along much more rapidly than would have been otherwise possible. But there were voices of concern. Legislators grumbled that the governors had been given too much power in the new organization. In consequence the compact was changed.

More and stronger protests came from other sectors, notably from higher education. There was no assurance that the several segments of higher education would be represented in decisions and recommendations (this concerned private as well as public institutions). Higher education was not dropped out of the compact, but concessions were made.

Most of these topics touch on the basic theme of this WICHE conference, the relationship between educators and public officials. And in this same area one finds the main success of the compact to date.

Chapter 6

The Compact for Education

by
Fred Harvey Harrington
President
University of Wisconsin

W hether one likes it or not, higher education and government are forever tied together—more closely than ever before in
American history. Since this is so, college and university administrators and elected officials, federal, state, and local, should get to
know each other a little better for their own good and for the good
of the republic.

This is a good starting point for a discussion of the Education
Commission of the States, set up under the new Compact for
Education. For if the compact has a contribution to make, it is
basically in the field of the interrelationship between education and
government.

The Compact: A Discussion of the Future

Note that I say "if." This is not meant to suggest doubt as to
the value of the Education Commission of the States. Rather the
intention is to suggest that any discussion of the compact must be
primarily a discussion of the future. The organization is formally
in existence; but it is not yet really off the ground.

This is a point that requires emphasis. Many think of the compact as already a going concern. After all, the organization meeting
in Kansas City in 1965 did have before it a full compact document. Then came formal creation of the Education Commission

of the States at a Chicago meeting in June 1966, with announcement that the compact had been officially approved by most of the states. Even before that, there was an announcement that the commission had an executive director, Wendell H. Pierce, superintendent of schools in Cincinnati. The delegates who gathered in Chicago chose permanent headquarters, Denver, and approved a batch of study topics proposed by the Interim Steering Committee.

All that sounds impressive. Impressive, too, are many of the strong statements that have been made about the venture. I have heard prominent public figures describe the compact as the great hope of the age, one of the most important developments of the twentieth century. I have heard other, equally prominent citizens, label it as one of the greatest threats to education in recent history.

As of this moment, both statements are rather doubtful. The compact is not as yet particularly important, either for good or for bad. It may be. It does have real promise of being useful, both to education and to state government. There is also a chance that it will damage existing institutions. But as of now the compact is not a major force.

The Fate of Great Expectations

What is the problem? Partly it is a matter of time and partly of expectations beyond the realm of likely results. The proper counsel now is to take the long view, and in doing so to be realistic about possible accomplishments.

To elaborate:

(1) It takes time to launch any organization. It takes a great deal of time to launch an organization designed to bring together elected officeholders, educators at all levels, and members of the general public. When fifty states are involved, and when formal ratification of an agreement is involved, the task assumes large proportions.

Take one angle only, legislative approval. By late summer 1966 thirty-seven—more than three-quarters—of the states had joined the compact. More than half, however, had done so by act of the governor. In nearly every case, approval by the legislature will be necessary for full participation, including payment of the state's financial contribution to the commission. Generally, approval will be forthcoming, but it will take time. Biennial odd-numbered-year sessions are still the rule. Which is a way of saying that many states could not move to legislative endorsement from the time of the Kansas City meeting in 1965 until 1967.

Setting up a staff also involves time, especially in these days of heavy competition for high-level talent. The man who organized the compact, former Governor Terry Sanford of North Carolina, was not available to carry on after the launching. The Interim Steering Committee of the Education Commission of the States was fortunate in securing the services of Ronald Moskowitz, a bright young Californian from Governor Brown's staff, to serve as associate director immediately after the Kansas City meeting. The search for an executive director moved along with reasonable speed, and in the spring of 1966 Wendell Pierce accepted the appointment. He could not, however, free himself from his responsibilities as school superintendent in Cincinnati until January 1967. The usual difficulties of securing the right sort of specialist assistants further complicated the time schedule.

None of this involved extraordinary delay. Rather, it is the normal story of a new office. But expectations for the compact were extremely high, largely because of the speed with which Governor Sanford had moved his program forward. There were some expressions of disappointment by the summer of 1966, especially in political circles ("What is happening?" "What are we going to get for our money?"). Chances are that there will be further comments of that sort before the Education Commission of the States can deliver much in the way of actual results. As progress becomes apparent, though, such statements should become less frequent.

(2) More important than the time schedule is the matter of realistic expectations. The language of the compact is very broad. It is so sweeping as to alarm many observers, a point on which I will comment later. Others have welcomed the strong phrases, seeing an opportunity to solve the problems of this generation. State officeholders and other citizens baffled by the complexity of educational needs are looking to this agency as one that can provide answers.

Perhaps it can—in time and in some measure. Unfortunately, many citizens are expecting too much. The compact may be able to do a great deal, but it probably cannot perform all the wonders.

Why? There are built-in limits. An educational commission of fifty states, with seven delegates from each, is large for efficient operation. Meetings will be infrequent, presumably once a year. Membership is bound to shift. It will be hard to arrange for a satisfactory exchange of views. It will be harder to reach significant agreement, with inexperienced delegates representing a wide range of views.

There will of course be a staff and a steering committee to get things ready for meetings of the commission. The steering committee, however, will be large (thirty-two members). Attendance promises to be a problem. With many different viewpoints represented and a shifting membership, progress may well be slow.

There is another limitation, money. The basic support of the education commission will come from state contributions. These will be large enough to support a substantial staff but not large enough to perform all the services that some expect. It should be possible to finance special studies with private foundation and federal government funds, but present budget guesses suggest a moderate-sized rather than a mammoth operation.

This is not said in criticism. The commission should be able to accomplish a good deal. Results are likely to be best if it does not try to do everything. It is important, however, to make those who hope for miracles realize that lesser achievements are worthwhile.

This may not be easy.

Enthusiasts have been over-estimating compact possibilities. Opponents have over-estimated the dangers. It may be, therefore, that if the education commission has limited rather than total success, fears and opposition will decline.

Which Directions Are the Right Ones?

The job now is to see that the organization does move, and in the right directions.

Which are those?

Toward better understanding and cooperation among educators, public officials, and citizens generally, without undermining satisfactory relations already in existence.

This point covers the whole of education, but I will confine my remarks to higher education.

Relations between government and higher education are anything but new. When we trace the history of the American university, we quote Thomas Jefferson, a politician, more than we quote any professional educator. We see that almost every one of the American contributions to education involves the closest relationship between government and campus: mass or universal education; the rise of research; the distinctively American phenomena of extension and public service, through which our higher education has carried learning beyond the classroom, library, and laboratory to the people.

As a land-grant institution, my own University of Wisconsin has depended on government funds for a century—has been supported by Congress and the state legislature for teaching, research, and public service.

Does this mean that we have been associated with politicians?

Of course we have. The territorial politicians started us, as part of the growth plan connected with the Wisconsin statehood movement. National political leaders, including President Abraham Lincoln, broadened us in the Civil War era by supporting agricultural and engineering studies. Before World War I their White House and congressional successors were enabling us to develop research and extension activities.

Soil and Seminar—Campus and Capitol

In turn we served the politicians by proving that their votes for education yielded good results. In my state the progressive era brought a new twist after 1900—the Wisconsin Idea, really a partnership of Campus and Capitol (soil and seminar, we called it, to show the tie of the university to the people). Professors went on loan to state government, served on state commissions, supplied ideas for social and economic legislation, and trained state officials.

Nor was that the end. World War I brought the beginnings of the same sort of partnership between the federal government and American universities. This was greatly expanded in and after World War II, especially in research. It became commonplace for professors to take leave and work for the federal government. Lately we have seen a sharp increase in university-Washington cooperation on problem-solving and action programs (poverty, community service, the Peace Corps, technical services to industry, to name a few). Meantime, there are new teaching-research-service partnerships between our campuses and foreign governments. And professors are working more closely with American city governments.

Inevitably this has brought professional educators into closer touch with elected officials. There has been some of this for a long time. The difference now is one of size and complexity. The operation is getting bigger, more expensive, more complicated. So we must work harder for understanding and cooperation.

Take the federal government. Washington support for higher education, formerly rather small, now exceeds two billion dollars a year. What is more, the federal higher education effort is increasingly broad. Not long ago it centered largely on research. Now there is a heavy involvement in teaching and service programs. Both public and private colleges and universities are affected. The total is not enormous by defense expenditure standards, but it is large enough to make national executive and legislative leaders very education-minded. And, since the two billions is a fifth of the nation's total higher education budget, college and university administrators realize that they must spend more and more time in Washington. A decade ago some of these administrators could not even name their congressmen. Now they can call them by their first names.

Although federal government developments get most of the news space, the state legislatures continue to provide more higher education money than does Congress. With the enrollment boom of the present generation, colleges and universities have desperately needed funds. Their spokesmen have had to appeal time and again to governors and legislators and to the general public. They ask for more and more money for existing institutions, more and more for new campuses, more and more for professional and graduate work.

The State and the Educator: Mutual Distrust?

Meanwhile governors and state legislatures have been caught in a tax squeeze. With the federal government absorbing most of the tax dollar, not enough is left for the states, just when they need maximum amounts for highways, for health and welfare, as well as for education. Constituents have resisted tax increases—and at the same time have demanded more educational opportunities. Caught between these conflicting pressures, legislators and governors have generally provided the needed appropriations. At the same time, they have come to examine institutional requests much more closely than before. They have hired budget analysts for this; they have set up all sorts of coordinating boards to make sure that the educational dollar is spent wisely.

There has always been strain in the relationship between educators and elected officeholders. The strain has increased in recent years. Some politicians have made a specialty of attacking higher education as unnecessarily expensive, as arrogant and unresponsive to public opinion, even as immoral and disloyal. In turn, some educators have denounced politicians as lacking in understanding, devoted to mediocrity rather than high quality, and determined to strip the institutions of higher education of their autonomy in matters large and small.

Fortunately, these judgments are not universal. Most college and university administrators realize that political leaders want to provide the best educational services possible. Most officeholders are proud of the institutions in their districts and like to think of themselves as supporters of education. Educators whom I meet are forever boasting of the backing they receive from their political representatives. Officeholders whom I meet are forever boasting of the high quality of the colleges and universities in their districts.

Obviously, then, there is a great deal on which to build; the building has already begun. Regional organizations like WICHE have brought educators and officeholders together, and the results have been excellent. City, state, and federal government officials increasingly rely on university advice and cooperation. Universities work more closely than ever before with every sort of government agency. This has become easier as legislative and executive departments have built up competent full-time staffs.

But there is much more to do. Misunderstandings are numerous. Suspicion remains. Along with cooperation there are charges of interference. Many public officials feel that they should have more control over higher education. Many university trustees and administrators fear that their institutions are losing their autonomy, that elected officials are making all the basic decisions.

How does the Compact for Education fit in here? To some it seems to point to an increase in political interference in educational matters. To others (and I include myself) it offers promise of improved relationships between educators and elected officeholders.

Conant: The Birth of an Idea

The story begins with James B. Conant's *Shaping Educational Policy,* published by McGraw-Hill Book Company in 1964. Conant found education in "disarray." He traced much of the trouble to local control of the schools and to competition for state legislative appropriations among the public colleges and universities. He felt that strengthening state departments of education could help some at the school level (as in New York). In higher education he found hope in coordinating committees and master plans (as in California). But more was needed if Americans were to wrestle effectively with junior college and vocational questions, with the problem of the underprivileged, with the need for uniformity in requirements for the Ph.D.

Since the national government does not control education, Conant maintained that there was need for cooperation between state officials and educational leaders across state lines. This was necessary, he said, to correct the "haphazard interaction" between these groups, to bring "some degree of order" into educational decisions. Why not a formal interstate compact for educational policy, he asked; why not work toward a "nationwide" policy in this field? Regional agreements had been successful. Why not try for more?

Shaping Educational Policy did not sell as well as Conant's famous *American High School Today.* Nor did it receive as much critical acclaim as had been showered on his *Slums and Suburbs.* Many educators disagreed with some or all of Conant's conclusions. There were those who felt that Conant should have given more attention to the advantages of diversity. Others feared that the compact proposal, if carried forward, would destroy or weaken useful relationships between politicians and school people built up through the years. One professor, M. M. Chambers, wrote a book-length answer to every point in the Conant study.

Shaping Educational Policy did, however, have many defenders; and, since it led to action, it is an important volume. It is worth reading for that reason alone—and for its many interesting suggestions. In my own re-reading I was struck by Conant's emphasis on the need for educators and elected officials to get together, to understand each other, to work together when at all possible.

Busy with many things, Conant did not intend to organize the interstate agreement proposed in *Shaping Educational Policy*. It was the Carnegie Corporation which took the next step. This foundation has supported all the Conant educational studies and has, of course, been interested in moving from study conclusions into action.

Sanford: The Birth of Reality

In this case Carnegie officials turned to Terry Sanford, North Carolina's "education governor," to carry forward the compact idea. The Carnegie and Danforth foundations provided the financing.

In the history of the formation of the compact, Sanford is as important as Conant. The proposal as contained in *Shaping Educational Policy* is very general. Sanford gave it shape. He did so in a remarkably short time, which is a tribute to his great ability, his drive, and his powers of persuasion.

When *Shaping Educational Policy* came out, John Gardner headed the Carnegie Corporation. Soon thereafter, as the compact began to take form, Gardner went to Washington as President Lyndon B. Johnson's Secretary of Health, Education, and Welfare. This led some to fear that the compact was really designed to secure general acceptance of federal education policies. Actually, it was nothing of the kind. Sanford is an enthusiastic believer in the importance of state action. When he took on the compact problem he was already involved in a Ford Foundation project on the role of the states. He and those who worked with him in

1965 seem to have hoped that the compact would result in interstate cooperation to make more effective use of state resources and also influence the direction of federal government activity in the education field.

Like Conant, Sanford believed in building bridges between educators and elected public officials. As governor of North Carolina he had seen these two groups working together harmoniously on projects of the Southern Regional Education Board. He was convinced that the same approach would work on a national scale.

Just how should this closer cooperation be arranged? Since the Conant book gave few clues as to how it should be done, the choice was left to Sanford. As a former state chief executive, he naturally inclined toward a structure that gave a prominent position to his old colleagues. Under the compact as he brought it forward, governors automatically belong to their state delegations at meetings of the Education Commission of the States, and most of the other delegates serve at the governor's pleasure. It developed that the Education Commission of the States would always be headed by a governor, and the state chief executives were guaranteed a strong position on the steering committee. At Sanford's urging, governors were out in front in support of the compact before its formal adoption; their leadership was apparent at the organization meeting in Kansas City in 1965.

There was certainly good reason for working with the governors. By doing so—and getting early backing from the Governors' Conference—Sanford was able to move the compact along much more rapidly than would otherwise have been possible. It is clear, too, that no interstate compact would have been possible without strong support from the governors. Besides, governors have a central role in educational planning. Nearly every one of them puts education at the top of his list of problems. Was it not right that they should have the key position?

Perhaps, but there were voices of concern.

Crisis: Who is to Lead?

Some concern was voiced by other elected officeholders. In one state the legislature refused to accept the compact after the governor had endorsed it. In others legislators grumbled that the governors had been given too much power in the new organization. To be sure, the compact provided that both houses of the legislatures would be represented on the state delegations at the annual meetings of the Education Commission of the States. But there was no formal assurance that the state legislative voice would be as strong as that of the governors on the steering committee, where many decisions would be made. The battle was clearly joined in California and other states, and national state legislative spokesmen like Unruh of California and McCarty of Oklahoma made their views known.

What to do? For legal and other reasons those who had drawn up the compact had vigorously opposed amending the original language. Every one could see, though, that legislative consent was necessary. To be sure, the compact was to go into effect when ten states had joined. Obviously, however, more were needed—for effective cooperation and because the states were to pay the bills after the initial (foundation-support) period.

In consequence, the compact was changed. The size of the steering committee was increased to thirty-two. Legislators were guaranteed representation equal to that of the governors (eight each, the remaining half being reserved for educators and other citizens).

Crisis: Should Higher Education Follow?

More and stronger protests came from other sectors, notably from higher education. The higher education complaints were not all owing to the place of the governors in the compact. Some were directed at the speed of organization. Sanford had been in touch with a number of educational associations before the Kansas City meeting and he had called some meetings for comment and discussion. Most college and university presidents, though, were caught by surprise when the compact was brought forward. Many felt that the new organization did not give enough consideration to the existence of regional organizations. Others said that the compact was not really needed (were there not enough organizations, enough meetings, enough studies already?). And there were comments on the absence of faculty voices in affairs of the Compact for Education.

Most important was the matter of representation. Since the governors controlled the makeup of the state delegations to the education commission, there was no assurance that the several segments of higher education would be represented in decisions and recommendations (this concerned private as well as public institutions). Presidents of state universities were of course accustomed to dealing with their governors and legislatures and coordinating committees. They were worried, however, about the possibility that the seven-man state delegations to the Education Commission of the States might become additional "state educational councils" back home, adding one more policy or review group to those already in existence.

Higher education opposition mounted after the Kansas City meeting. It was especially strong in the National Association of State Universities and Land-Grant Colleges. This group proposed that higher education be omitted from the compact; or, that failing, that the Education Commission of the States establish a special advisory committee for higher education.

Concerned, the Interim Steering Committee of the compact gave a good deal of attention to higher education attitudes in 1965-66. There was spirited debate at the New York and Santa Fe meetings of the Interim Steering Committee, with some sharp criticism and some strong defense of the views of college and university spokesmen. Higher education was not dropped out of the compact. But concessions were made:

(1) It was agreed that the seven-man state delegations to the Education Commission of the States would be just that, and would not function as educational councils back home.

(2) The Interim Steering Committee agreed that there would be a special Higher Education Advisory Committee, to be nominated by the American Council on Education. This advisory committee was set up in the summer of 1966 and first met in September. It chose as its chairman President Elvis Stahr of Indiana University. Stahr had strongly opposed the compact. But, now that it was in existence, he was willing to work with the Interim Steering Committee in the interests of higher education. A number of his colleagues shared his attitude.

Many had feared that the governors would dominate the compact. Actually, a main problem was getting these busy executives to attend meetings of the commission and its steering committee. In an effort to boost gubernatorial attendance the Interim Steering Committee decided that absent governors could send representatives but that these substitutes could not vote. The result is not yet certain.

At its Chicago meeting in June 1966, the Education Commission of the States approved several study topics of interest to higher education: the junior college question; state-wide coordination of higher education; vocational and technical education; and the improvement of communication between government officials and others interested in education. As can be seen, most of these topics touch on the basic theme of this WICHE conference, the relationship between educators and public officials. And in this same area one finds the main success of the compact to date. That is to be found in the mixing of educators, public officials, and other citizens. The value of this was particularly apparent in the meetings of the Interim Steering Committee.

If that spirit is retained, and if the compact puts emphasis on this cooperation, we may all be the gainers.

**See Section VI in the back of this book
for annotated bibliography of related materials.**

Precis

The University and the State: A Comparative Study

The greatest degree of separation of the university from the body politic is found—today almost exclusively—in Oxford and Cambridge, which are still self-governing societies of academics. This is not the American way.

Almost without exception in the United States, the government of colleges and universities is placed in the hands of lay boards of trustees. And, increasingly, public colleges and universities in the United States have been subjected to restricted controls by state finance, personnel, and purchasing departments. State governments should determine only the resources available to the university and leave the effective expenditure of those funds to the institution.

In spite of the need for freedom from budgetary controls, public institutions must not be insensitive to the social, economic, and cultural needs of the people who support them. And, if universities are to perform only limited functions at the apex of a public system of higher education, then they should encourage the creation or development of other institutions serving other significant social needs.

Unless institutions or responsible educational bodies themselves lay down the outlines of a responsive, responsible, and comprehensive system of higher education, the government will play a far more aggressive role in influencing or controlling both the direction and the operation of colleges and universities. State-wide coordination is developing rapidly, but there is no evidence of the effectiveness of its various types.

Problems of state-wide planning and coordination are intricate enough, but new implications are on the horizon in the United States and elsewhere. The President and the Congress look upon colleges and universities as instruments of national power, as prime contributors to economic growth, as suppliers of specialists for government service, and as promoters of human welfare.

Some of the dangers of allying the university with government are obvious. Others are subtle. In this interchange the universities have almost certainly lost some of their prerogative to criticize, some of their freedom to speak out on controversial political and economic issues.

Chapter 7

The University and the State:
A Comparative Study

by
T. R. McConnell
Professor of Higher Education
University of California at Berkeley

W riting on "The Politics of Education," Lawrence A. Cremin, the eminent educational historian, pointed to a tension that has characterized popular education from the beginning.

> On the one hand there is the prerogative of the public to set policy, determine direction, and fix support: we speak of public *control,* not merely public sponsorship or public influence. On the other hand, there is the prerogative of the teaching profession to govern its own work, set standards, and determine the nature of teaching practice: the teacher is committed to teaching truth as he sees it and to following the truth wherever it leads. Recognizing this tension, the late Charles Beard used to argue that a democratic society should support schools which should then be left free to criticize the society that supports them.[1]

Cremin pointed out, however, that the lower schools have seldom enjoyed genuine freedom for social criticism. Only colleges and universities have won this prerogative, and even today their independence is by no means universally or completely secure. Weaker institutions are often subservient to political forces, religious pressures, or coercion by conservative private interests. The more distinguished institutions, large or small, on the other hand, have governing boards and administrative officers which protect faculty members with liberal or even leftist attitudes. Summarizing their data on the "Vulnerability and Strength of the Superior College," Lazarsfeld and Thielens reached the following conclusions:

The higher the quality of a college, the larger its proportion of permissive (liberal) social scientists.

The higher the quality, the stronger the pressures and attacks from the off-campus community.

The higher the quality of the school, the better the performance of the administration in defending the academic freedom of its social scientists.

The same authors then asked:

If the more distinguished colleges are more subject to pressure and more frequently the scene of controversial incidents, how is it, nevertheless, that their administrations perform better by all of our criteria, including the protection given social scientists?

They answered the question as follows:

For the most part the individuals chosen as trustees are selected because they are successful in their own enterprises . . . . If they are responsible for a college, they want it to have prestige, so they appoint presidents who they hope will make their regime "successful," without going too deeply into the existing academic implications of the idea. The president, in turn, will build up a staff whose men and women command the respect of their peers and live up to the prevailing norms of the teaching profession. We have shown that a permissive atmosphere is a part of these norms . . . .

Even if they themselves have conservative attitudes, it will be exactly those administrators who have built up successful colleges who will have the strongest personal and professional involvement in the prestige of their institutions, and be least willing to sacrifice good teachers in the interests of possibly temporary cycles in idealogical mood . . . . The more successful he has been in building up the prestige of his college, the more likely he will be to protect it now against the pressures upon it.[2]

Attempts by both politicians and trustees to restrict or censure free teaching and expression by faculty members probably impinge more often on tax-supported institutions than upon those which are privately financed. Let it not be supposed, however, that privately controlled colleges and universities invariably escape attacks on academic freedom. From my experience in both publicly and privately supported institutions, I conclude that both are subject to pressure from powerful, often subtle, external forces, although the form and origin of the encroachment may differ. The fact that countervailing forces play upon the two groups of colleges and universities strengthens both in fending off attacks on their freedom. The dual system of public and private higher education in the

United States strengthens the independence and integrity of the whole.

Speaking of a trend toward monolithic control of American higher education, Logan Wilson declared recently:

> As a firm believer in a dual system of higher education, I contend that this trend toward a monolithic scheme is neither desirable nor necessary. In view of recent developments in the control of public higher education, it seems to me more vital than ever before to strengthen the capabilities of private institutions.[3]

Important as the private sector may be, however, the growing public, and especially federal, support for private institutions blurs the distinction between the public and private sectors, and threatens to subject the latter to political influence. I shall return to this point later.

Separation of the University and the Body Politic

One device for protecting the university's prerogative for social criticism is to insulate the institution from control by a government ministry or from *direct* popular control. The greatest degree of separation of the university from the body politic is found—today almost exclusively—in Oxford and Cambridge, which are still self-governing societies of academics, although both universities, as distinct from their constituent colleges, get most of their support from the state. Although they are formally self-governing, these ancient universities have not been completely insulated from external influences. Royal Commissions have demanded reforms; they are subject to minimal controls by the University Grants Committee; and recently the Robbins Committee on Higher Education directed some sharp criticisms toward Oxford's organizational structure, administrative processes, and educational affairs. So pointed were these shafts that Oxford, fearing, it is said, that the Robbins Report might lead to the appointment of another Royal Commission, hastened to appoint its own committee to appraise its operations and to recommend desirable changes. This was the Franks Committee, which recently issued a two-volume report which proposed that the university should streamline its structure and administration but retain its self-government. The report explicitly vetoed the Robbins proposal to add laymen to the university's governing body.[4]

Academic self-government is not the American way. Almost without exception the government of colleges and universities in the United States is placed in the hands of lay boards of trustees which are invested by charter or legislation with supreme authority over their institutions, although the boards may, and usually do, delegate all or parts of their authority to their own officers and committees, the president and other administrative officials of the institution, and the faculty.

Governing boards of public institutions enjoy a measure of independence from political pressure by virtue of the fact that the members are appointed for relatively long, overlapping terms, a procedure which makes it difficult for a single governor to control the board's composition.

Terms of office, it may be noted, can be *too* long. Members of the Board of Regents of the University of California are appointed for sixteen-year terms, and in the past were often reappointed. It is not surprising that the sign which greeted you as you entered the campus is both literally and figuratively true:

PROPERTY OF THE REGENTS OF THE UNIVERSITY OF CALIFORNIA
The regents of this university have been notorious for intervening in administrative affairs which should be delegated to the executive officers and faculties of the institution. Fortunately, limited progress in this delegation has recently been made.

In the overwhelming number of cases, the members of governing boards of publicly controlled institutions are appointed by the governor alone, or with the concurrence of the senate. It is widely believed that appointive boards are less susceptible to political pressure than are those whose members are elected by the people. In Illinois, where the governing board of the state university is elected, political partisanship has been tempered over a long period by the practice in both major political parties of accepting candidates nominated by the university's alumni association. This policy, however, has not always prevailed. It was a politically nominated board member, a former famous football star, who introduced the motion of no-confidence which led some years ago to the resignation of President George L. Stoddard. There are some political scientists and educators who believe that public universities should be directly responsible to the electorate and thus more intimately accountable to the people. But a much larger proportion of students of administration believe that the indirect form of representation is more effective in protecting institutions from the vagaries and impulses of the public will.

Faculty Representation on the Governing Board

As noted previously, the governing boards of public colleges and universities in the United States are almost invariably composed of laymen. The instances in which faculty members sit on governing bodies of their own institutions are extremely rare. One of the exceptions was the University of Buffalo before it became a part of the State University of New York. There was no formal system of faculty representation even at Buffalo. However, the alumni of the university, from their own roster, elected one-third of the voting members of the governing board, and while I was chancellor they could and did elect administrative officers or faculty members. Indoctrinated as I was with American practice, I looked on this situation with some misgivings. I must say, however, that experience dissipated my doubt about the desirability of having members of the university's staff among my employers. I concluded that their presence was a valuable means of communication in both directions between the staff and the governors. The opportunity for an interchange of attitudes and ideas led to a better understanding of the nature of the university on the part of the lay members, and to a better appreciation of the relationship of the university to its public on the part of the faculty and administrative staff.

The American Association of University Professors has long pressed for faculty representation on governing boards, and I should like to see the principle widely adopted. The practice of the English civic universities in including faculty members on the court has proved its value, and the seven new universities have followed the custom. As the colleges of advanced technology become universities, members of the staff are also included in their governing bodies.

There is pressure in some of the universities in Ontario, where I visited recently, for faculty representation. The faculty of one institution, in fact, wanted a majority of the places on the governing board. This seems to me to be going too far; it would vitiate the principle of lay control, which, in spite of the abuses to which it has been subjected from time to time or place to place, seems to me to be essentially sound. Nevertheless, faculty membership on the boards of public institutions would, in my judgment, greatly improve the liaison between the people and the government on the one hand, and the colleges and universities on the other, and make the boards more effective buffers between the university and the state.

State Intervention in University Affairs

Public colleges and universities in the United States have been increasingly subjected to restrictive controls by state finance, personnel, and purchasing departments. Growing governmental control over the fiscal operations and, through fiscal intervention, over educational affairs as well, led in 1957 to the appointment of a Committee on Government and Higher Education to study the changing relationships between state governments and public institutions of higher education. This committee's report documented a growing threat to the corporate autonomy of state colleges and universities through close supervision by various state officials—budget officers, comptrollers, purchasing agents, and legislative auditors. This intervention, said the committee, amounted in many instances to a usurpation of the responsibility of those in whom it was legally vested.[5]

Most public institutions or systems of higher education must submit their appropriation requests to a state department of finance for review and final incorporation in the governor's executive budget for submission to the legislature. The Committee on Government and Higher Education found that state finance officers frequently made decisions, not alone on the general level of support which should be afforded higher education in competition with other governmental services, but also on specific items of proposed expenditure involving such fundamental matters as educational program, faculty salaries, and admission policies. The committee passed forthright judgment on this practice when it said:

> Viewed from a management perspective alone, it violates the canons of sound administration for a college governing board to be vested with legal and public responsibility for the conduct of educational affairs, while the real decision-making power resides at some remote spot in the state bureaucracy. The maxim that

authority should be commensurate with responsibility is grossly violated on a campus where routine decisions on financial matters are in fact made by a state official. Carried to an extreme, as it has been in some places, such a system of remote control denies to governing boards and college presidents the power they are intended and entitled to have. In such a situation, public officials who may be ill-equipped to make educational decisions are moved into a position where they govern higher education without bearing any visible responsibility for its success or failure.[6]

One of the best examples of the assumption of the prerogatives of a responsible governing board by the officials—and often subordinate rather than principal officers—of an executive budget agency may be found in the administration of the California state college system. Three surveys have criticized the state finance department for such practices as requiring the institutions to submit line item budgets for approval, making a pre-audit of expenditures, and retaining control over transfer of funds from one item or classification to another.

In the *Restudy of the Needs of California in Higher Education,* published in 1958, I wrote:

> . . . it is recommended that the State Department of Finance discontinue its pre-audit of expenditures after the budget for the state colleges has been approved and the legislative appropriation has been made. It is recommended, further, that the state college governing board be authorized to transfer funds from one item to another in the current operating budget, and to release funds from reserve or contingency categories as educational and administrative needs and operating efficiency dictate.

The Master Plan for Higher Education in California made the same proposals in 1960, and the Coordinating Council for Higher Education, which was created pursuant to the master plan, has strongly pressed for appropriate fiscal authority for the state college system. Nevertheless, the State Department of Finance has persisted in its restrictive controls instead of authorizing the state colleges to establish a modern system of performance budgeting, and so has continued to impose on the institutions an inflexible, stultifying, and in my judgment, a fiscally inefficient form of operation.

Appropriators and Spenders: There Is a Difference

The California Coordinating Council has repeatedly recommended that the trustees of the state college system should be given a large degree of flexibility in determining how appropriated funds can be most effectively used in carrying out the functions and programs of the institutions; more specifically, that a budget built around purposes and programs replace one composed of detailed line items; that the pre-auditing of expenditures be abandoned; that the legislature make a single appropriation for operations to the state college system; and that the trustees then allocate financial resources to individual colleges.

The California Coordinating Council and the state college system have stated that the system should devise methods of effective program evaluation and efficient financial management, together with adequate reporting, plus a post-audit of expenditures, as means of accountability for the performance of its purposes and the stewardship of its financial resources. The governor recently directed all state agencies, including those concerned with higher education, to go to a program budget, beginning in 1967-68. This is encouraging progress.

The legislative analyst recently recommended, and in 1966 the legislature approved, a limited transfer of fiscal authority to the state college system. It is to be hoped that both the legislature and the finance department will accept the other recommendations of the coordinating council, the master plan, the previously expressed legislative intent to give the trustees authority commensurate with their responsibility, and modern methods of budgeting and administration that stress the effective accomplishment of mission rather than the limitation of expenditures.[7]

Certain state universities, including those in California, Minnesota, and Michigan, have a special constitutional status which, it has been said, makes them a fourth arm of the government. These universities usually possess full power over the expenditure of legislative appropriations. The autonomy of the University of California was established in the section of the state constitution which begins as follows:

> The University of California shall constitute a public trust, to be administered by the existing corporation known as "The Regents of the University of California," with full powers of organization and government subject only to such legislative control as may be necessary to insure compliance with the terms of the endowments of the University and the security of its funds.

The section provides further that:

> . . . said corporation shall also have all the powers necessary or convenient for the effective administration of its trust . . . and to delegate to its committees or to the faculty of the University, or to others, such authority or functions as it may deem wise . . . .

No public institution, whether it possesses constitutional autonomy or not, can or should treat the legislature in cavalier fashion. So long as it must return to the legislature each year or each biennium, an institution is fundamentally accountable to the lawmaking body. If a university secured additional support for specific purposes, such as new educational programs, additional staff, or higher faculty salaries, it would divert funds from these to other purposes only under the most extraordinary circumstances, and would properly have to justify its action the next time it approached the legislature for its operating budget. Thus, constitutional autonomy does not absolve a university from governmental accountability. However, responsibility and accountability do not require an institution to surrender to state executive officers the right to make decisions concerning the means by which it strives to attain its academic goals.

The fundamental distinction between appropriate and inappropriate fiscal controls by government agencies was stated by Arthur Naftalin when he was commissioner of administration for the State of Minnesota. Naftalin had been a professor of political science at the University of Minnesota before he entered the state government. As quoted in the report of the Committee on Government and Higher Education, he said:

> I should divide the problem of fiscal control over state-supported higher education into two parts. First, there is the initial question of which section of the state's resources should be devoted to higher education, and second, the expenditure and internal allocation of the state support once it has been voted. With respect to the first stage, I believe this is wholly, appropriately, and inescapably within the jurisdiction of the governor and the state legislature . . . . But with respect to the second stage, once the elected representatives have spoken, fiscal control should become the responsibility of the academy itself, as represented and symbolized by the regents or trustees or college board. It should be their responsibility to determine how the limited resources available shall be distributed among the infinite number of competing academic needs. To impose upon this process the will and direction of state fiscal officers constitutes an encroachment that is potentially extremely dangerous.[8]

In spite of the warning of the Committee on Government and Higher Education, a new investigation would show, I feel certain, that state agencies have strengthened their detailed fiscal control even over public institutions that presumably possess constitutional autonomy. For example, by reviewing specific budget items, the State Department of Finance has tended to erode the autonomy and authority of the University of California. If my memory serves me correctly, about ten years ago the university submitted a list of building priorities in requesting appropriations for capital purposes. The State Department of Finance revised the priorities according to its own lights which, with all due respect to the intelligence of the officers concerned, could hardly be as bright as the lights of those intimately involved with the university's development and integrity. Since that episode, the surveillance over the university's operations and development has grown steadily. Both the finance department and the legislature have in effect eliminated or altered line items in proposed budgets.

In preparing the executive budget, the finance department has on occasion questioned the academic staffing structure, e.g., the proportion of faculty at the several ranks, of a particular department. This review, it is true, has occurred before the legislature made the university's appropriation. But one wonders how soon the same kind of surveillance may be exercised *after* operating funds have been appropriated.

State funding of the university is on a monthly reimbursement basis. Not infrequently the finance department raises questions about the propriety of specific expenditures. To date, I believe, these questions have involved supply and expense items, rather than personnel costs. Again, however, one wonders when the review will extend to academic and non-academic personnel items. It may be argued that surveillance of expenditures through the reimbursement technique is a post-audit. Perhaps technically it is; in any event, it is a swift one.

The legislature last year excised an item of $100,000 for support of the University of California Press. If the state had to cut the university's request by $100,000, it should have left to the university the decision as to where the sum should be saved. From the same budget request, the lawmakers cut the item for teaching assistants in the amount of $600,000 and reduced by $400,000 the provision for remission of out-of-state tuition for graduate students who met certain academic requirements. These measures supposedly did not refer to the university's mission or programs. They did, however, seriously hamper the university in mobilizing the means to carry out its recognized roles. Again, the legislature should have determined the resources to be made available to the university and then have left to the institution the effective expenditure of the funds. Unless the University of California stubbornly resists the trend toward more detailed budgetary control from the statehouse, it will soon become politically subservient and its constitutional autonomy will become a hollow form. It will rapidly retrogress toward the unhappy situation of the state colleges.

The Social, Cultural, and Economic Needs of the Body Politic

Although public institutions should be free from restrictive budgetary controls, they must not be insensitive to the social, economic, and cultural needs of the people who support them. In the first article of the workbook for this conference, the author pointed to a difficult dilemma:

> . . . the need of independence for an educational institution from the source of its sustenance . . . this independence must be achieved in such a fashion that the institution doesn't isolate itself from reality and destroy its usefulness through ever-narrowing scholasticism.[9]

Sir Eric Ashby, master of Clare College at Cambridge, ran into the same dilemma. He said:

> The arguments for university autonomy, like the arguments for academic freedom, are weakened by querulous appeals to tradition and privilege. The only effective argument is the pragmatic one. A system of higher education, like an airline, is a highly technical organization. If experts are not allowed to run it without interference from the state, it will collapse. The only effective policy, therefore, is for universities, like airlines, to be left to manage their own affairs.

But then Sir Eric ran into a predicament. He conceded:

> The general difficulty is that the state undoubtedly has the right to make certain demands on its public services, including its system of higher education, and to expect these demands to be met.[10]

Considering possible governmental prerogatives, President Murray G. Ross of York University, Toronto, in his recent annual report, excerpts from which are reproduced in our workbook, posed

99

such questions as the following: Is it not appropriate for the government, either through its legislative or executive branches, to determine how many students publicly controlled colleges and universities should admit and what standards should be used in selecting them, what professional schools to establish and how many professionals to train, what buildings and equipment should be provided, what salaries should be paid to faculty and staff, what the distribution of faculty ranks should be, and what public services the university should perform?[11] Presumably Sir Eric would reply that it is not appropriate for the government to make final decisions on any of these matters, for he quoted Justice Frankfurter to this effect:

> It is the business of a university to provide that atmosphere which is most conducive to speculation, experiment, and creation. It is an atmosphere in which there prevail "the four essential freedoms" of a university—to determine for itself on academic grounds who may teach, what may be taught, how it shall be taught, and who may be admitted to study.[12]

Speaking on May 9, 1966, at a conference held by the Center for the Study of Democratic Institutions, Sir Eric admitted that the universities of his country, pursuing the "four freedoms," have denied the opportunity for higher education to tens of thousands of British children who deserve to have one. He also observed that Flexner, reflecting the conservative tradition of the British universities, had been mistaken in issuing ". . . Jeremiads about the introduction of journalism and business studies into American universities." Sir Eric went on: "I believe that to admit into the college curriculum new professional schools on our terms—the terms of the faculty, not of the legislature or the alumni—is an essential obligation of universities. But, let it be emphasized, on our terms, for we are the experts . . . ."[13]

My answer, too, is that the public university, not the state, should determine policy on such matters as whom to admit, what and how to teach, whom to appoint to the faculty and staff, and how much to pay them. This is not to say that the university should be insensitive to social needs. It is to say that the university must distinguish which of these needs it is appropriate for it to serve. If it responds to every strong pressure for some form of training, research, or public service, it will often find itself serving short-range goals rather than those of far-reaching significance.[14]

Not only should the public university eschew short-range goals; it should decide what functions it will perform *qua* university, and leave to other institutions a wide range of educational activities which are necessary in the public interest, but which are inappropriate to an institution which is the capstone of a public system of higher education. I have proposed elsewhere that the major American state universities should in fact become institutions of learning of the highest grade, and that they should concentrate their resources and programs on advanced undergraduate, professional, and graduate education; on research; and on related levels of public service.[15]

Felt Needs: The Responsibilities of Others

If universities are to perform limited functions at the apex of a public system of higher education, they have the obligation, it seems to me, to encourage the creation or development of other institutions serving other significant social needs. It was with this obligation in mind that I said that the major state universities should transfer their junior college functions to junior colleges, and that they should encourage the development of public regional four-year institutions offering instruction in liberal studies and selected professions, and, I would now add, appropriate programs of postgraduate instruction. Such a system of higher education has been developed most fully, perhaps, in California.

The University of California, in company with Stanford University, has long supported the development, expansion, and improvement of community colleges, and the University of California, through the California Coordinating Council, is cooperating with the state college system in developing a network of interrelated institutions performing both common and differential functions. Certain other states are now moving rapidly to bring a differentiated pattern of higher institutions into being and into productive coordination.

In Britain, on the other hand, the universities have until now maintained a monopoly on the awarding of degrees, and they have stubbornly protected their elite position in the whole structure of post-secondary education. ". . . by putting on the market, as it were, only Lincolns and no Fords, we have not fulfilled adequately our loyalty to contemporary society," is the way Sir Eric Ashby put it. Sir Eric went on to confess:

In our present social climate I don't believe excellence can be safeguarded (as we have tried to safeguard it in Britain) by keeping mediocrity out of higher education. This is simply unrealistic. I believe it must be safeguarded as you are trying to in America, by the peaceful coexistence of mediocrity and excellence. They have—after all—got to coexist elsewhere in society, and it is an educational commonplace that Gresham's Law does not hold for college degrees; indeed mediocrity is improved by association with excellence. Fords do not drive Lincolns off the market.[16]

I do not like Sir Eric's reference to "mediocrity and excellence." As a matter of fact, his use of the word "mediocrity" is inconsistent with his statement that quality has to do with the integrity of an educational enterprise, with an institution's or an individual's own purposes and performance.[17]

In stating that Gresham's Law does not hold for college degrees, Sir Eric implied that British higher education should abandon its attempt to maintain the equivalence of degrees (although they are almost certainly not as equivalent as is often assumed).

I shall discuss later the bearing of the abandonment of the doctrine of equivalence in connection with the development of a non-university sector of higher education in Britain.

In an address on April 27, 1965, which was afterwards officially released by the Ministry, the Secretary of State for Education and Science created no small amount of consternation and opposition in British university circles by announcing that the government planned to establish what has come to be known as a binary system of higher education. By implication, Secretary Crosland charged that the universities had been insensitive, or at least unresponsive, to social requirements, and declared that consequently "a substantial part of the higher education system should be under social control, and directly responsible to social needs." He also asserted that in Britain there "is an ever-increasing need and demand for vocational, professional, and industrially-based courses in higher education" which "cannot be fully met by the universities" and therefore "requires a separate sector, with a separate tradition and outlook within the higher education system." Mr. Crosland went on to say:

> . . . a system based on the ladder concept must inevitably depress and degrade both morale and standards in the non-university sector. If the universities have a "class" monopoly of degree-giving,

and if every college which achieves high standards moves auto-matically into the University Club, then the residual public sector becomes a permanent poor relation perpetually deprived of its brightest ornaments, and with a permanently and openly inferior status. This must be bad for morale, bad for standards, and pro-ductive only of an unhealthy competitive mentality.

Mr. Crosland also stated that it was essential to establish "a vocationally oriented non-university sector which is degree-giving and with an appropriate amount of postgraduate work with oppor-tunities for learning comparable with those of the universities, and giving a first-class professional training. Let us now move away from our snobbish cast-ridden hierarchial obsession with university status."

The annoyance and even the anger of some sections of the British university community are not surprising in view of some of Secretary Crosland's language and imputations. Although he may now be somewhat rueful about the manner in which he put his points, he has not deserted the substance of his case. At the end of May, a "white paper" from the Department of Education and Science appeared under the title of "A Plan for Polytechnics and Other Colleges: Higher Education in the Further Education System."[18]

The "Polytechnics": The English Reasoning

The "white paper" announced that the Department of Education and Science would designate a number of polytechnics (perhaps thirty) which would concentrate wholly or mainly on students of age eighteen and over pursuing courses of higher education. In addition, certain specialized colleges, such as those in commerce, music, and art, may be designated as parts of the system or may be incorporated in the polytechnics. The department also an-nounced that it would add no new polytechnics to the list for ten years. Presumably, the department believes that by freezing the status of institutions of further education it can stop what Mr. Crosland referred to in his speech as a "continuous rat-race" to "ape the universities above," with the consequence of almost "in-evitable failure to achieve the diversity in higher education which contemporary society needs." At the same time, the department announced that there would be no new universities or accessions to university status during the same decade.

The polytechnics will not be empowered, in the beginning at any rate, to award their own degrees. But the traditional monopoly of the universities over degrees will nevertheless be broken. Students who satisfactorily complete courses approved by the Council for National Academic Awards, which was recently created by Royal Charter, will be granted degrees by the council. The CNAA is the successor to the National Council for Technological Awards, which had been established to award the Diploma in Technology (as a presumably equivalent substitute for degrees) to students who were graduated from the Colleges of Advanced Technology or approved advanced courses in certain technical colleges.

In an effort to assure equivalence in quality with university degrees, the National Council for Technological Awards set very high standards for the "Dip. Tech." Apparently the CNAA plans to follow the doctrine (which, as I said above, is part fiction) of equivalence in standards (if not in content and emphasis) in approving courses for degrees in the polytechnics. In my judgment, this is undesirable. It will be necessary for Britain to educate a wider band of students, so far as level and type of aptitudes, abilities, and achievement are concerned. To award degrees to such students will do something, at least, to make attendance at other than university institutions of higher education socially acceptable to students, faculties, parents, and employers.[19]

The universities are disturbed by the creation of another system of higher education for several reasons. First of all, they believe that the government has not provided sufficient funds for capital and recurrent expenditures to enable them to meet the enrollment targets to which they are committed under the Robbins Report, and they are now fearful that the development of the polytechnics will divert resources to these institutions at the expense of university development and improvement. It is widely recognized that the Robbins Report underestimated the demand for higher education, and the universities are afraid that they will be held to the Robbins enrollment predictions and that the surplus of students will be directed to the polytechnics where, as some put it, the students will be educated "on the cheap." The universities thus envision a plateau of little expansion and limited development until the next big enrollment bulge appears in the Seventies.

The most thoughtful critics of the dual system of higher education object to it on grounds of divisiveness and rigidity. The bifurcated system appeared from Secretary Crosland's speech to create a strict separation between the elite "autonomous sector" composed of the universities, and a "public sector" composed of institutions of higher education presumably more responsive to social and economic needs.

Sir Peter Venables said:

> This policy has such an air of rigidity and of establishing a deep dichotomy in higher education as to raise serious concern about frustrating the national evolution of institutions and of fruitful relations between them . . . . A higher education policy of "separate but equal" may be attractive at first sight, but it is at least possible that long-term needs can only be met by a unitary system of higher education.[20]

The rigid separation between the "public" and "autonomous" sectors implied in Secretary Crosland's address seemed to forestall plans for the development of higher educational complexes in Manchester, Sussex, and Birmingham. Plans had been under way to associate in various ways the University of Manchester, the University's Institute of Science and Technology, the John Dalton Technical College, and colleges of education, art, and music, all of which are located relatively close together in a redeveloped section of the city of Manchester.

The new University of Sussex has been built four miles out of Brighton. Half-way between Brighton and the university there is a regional college of technology, working almost entirely at degree level, and across the road from the university are the new buildings of the teacher training college. In Brighton the College of Art offers a large amount of advanced-level work. Plans have been under way to relate and coordinate the work of these institutions, including the development of cooperative courses leading to both baccalaureate and advanced degrees of the university.

In Birmingham the new University of Aston, created out of the College of Advanced Technology, is located in the center of the city. Beside it are the new buildings of the Colleges of Art and Commerce, both of which emphasize advanced courses. A new student union serves all three institutions. Arrangements have already been made and approved for affiliation between the College of Art and the University of Aston in a cooperative program in architecture leading to a degree of the university. The future will almost certainly bring proposals for other courses leading to degrees of the same university.

There is a widespread fear that the effort of the Department of Education and Science to bring a summary stop to the "rat-race" for university status and to establish a second sector of higher education leading toward degrees of the Council for National Academic Awards will forestall fruitful relationships among different but interdependent institutions of higher education. Such relationships, it was said, might encourage experimentation and innovation. They might also promote greater flexibility in meeting the needs of students, for example, by enabling them to move more easily from one institution to another or from one program to another according to their interests, abilities, and aspirations. Such movement is now very difficult.

The fears of the universities have been somewhat allayed by a paragraph in the "white paper" which stated that "there will be great educational benefit in close academic and other relationships between the polytechnics and other colleges engaged in higher education . . . within the surrounding area," and that the Secretary of State is anxious that "mutually advantageous links with the universities shall be developed through sharing of staff, joint use of communal and other facilities and in other ways." Although this statement was cynically received in some university quarters, others accepted it at face value. In commenting on this varied response, the Secretary of State has declared that the statement was a sincere one.

It seems clear that if a flexible system of higher education is to be attained in Britain, rigid stratification, either horizontal or vertical, should be avoided. What Britain needs is not a less flexible system of higher education, but one whose parts are more interdependent and articulated. It remains to be seen whether stratification or flexibility materializes. Interdependence and articulation require the coordination of the elements of a diversified system of higher education. At the moment no scheme for collaboration and coordination at national, regional, and local levels between the university system and the polytechnics and specialized colleges has been devised or even proposed, although the Secretary of State has said recently that appropriate advisory bodies will be consulted when the new polytechnics are designated. The success of the whole enterprise of higher education in Britain may depend in the long run, not on the development of a unitary or monolithic system of higher education, but on a sensible division of responsibilities, cooperative planning in the development both of particular institutions and groups of institutions, and the evolution of a *pattern* of colleges and universities which reflects both the variation in students' interests, abilities, and aspirations, and the diversity of society's social, economic, and cultural needs.

The "Polytechnics": A Warning for All

The creation of a second, separate system of British higher education teaches a clear lesson. Unless institutions or responsible educational bodies themselves lay down the outlines of a responsive, responsible, and comprehensive system of higher education, the government will play a far more aggressive role in influencing or controlling both the direction and the operation of colleges and universities. After a visit to Britain in 1964, I predicted that the government would intervene more decisively not only in the development of higher education as a whole, but also in the affairs of the universities themselves. My visit in 1966 revealed that this prediction had come true. Not only had the Department of Education and Science established a second segment of higher education but, under government pressure, the University Grants Committee was conducting a cost study in the universities, the results of which will almost certainly be used by the government in allocating resources to the universities in competition with the other sector of higher education. This is only one example of the way in which the government, or the government through the University Grants Committee, will invade the universities' privileged sanctuary.

The University Grants Committee: A Buffer Zone

Leaving aside for the moment the desirability of a dual system of higher education in Britain, let us turn to the effectiveness of university coordination there. The instrument of financial liaison between the universities and the newly established Secretary of

107

State for Science and Education is still the University Grants Committee. The UGC, a large proportion of whose members are academics, has been a highly successful buffer between the universities and the main source of their support. In spite of the fact that the British universities have become almost entirely dependent on the state for funds, they have managed to maintain an amazing degree of autonomy. In the minds of some British critics the universities have in fact maintained too great a degree of independence with too little accountability to the government and too little responsiveness to the social, economic, and cultural needs of the country. The UGC has been a good buffer against governmental intervention in university affairs, but it has been relatively ineffective in long-range planning. As I have said elsewhere:

> Whatever direction the Committee has given the universities has had to be exerted gingerly. As one official in a position to know expressed it, the coordination the UGC has attained has been accomplished either through the most delicate negotiation and persuasion, earmarked grants (which the universities have disliked), or outright bribery. The result is a system of higher education far short of the nation's needs. Whether the government would have financially underwritten a bolder or more adequate national system of universities is admittedly doubtful, but in any event neither the UGC nor the universities themselves have ever come forth with any such plan. It is doubtful that they would ever voluntarily do so.[21]

Although the full-time staff of the UGC has recently been considerably expanded, it is still inadequate to the complicated task of planning and coordination. The general stance of the UGC has also produced a deficit in leadership. When I was in Britain in the summer of 1964, I could find little recognition at the UGC, or among the heads of the universities, for that matter, that there will have to be purposeful planning of a system of higher education that is most unlikely to take form through voluntary means; that there will have to be more prudent allocation of resources if the increasing number of youth qualified for higher education are to be served and if the needs for specialized manpower are to be met; that higher education will have to become more responsive to social and economic conditions; and, finally, that the basis for planning and for allocating resources is continuing research.

In 1966 I found more concern about the allocation of resources, for which the cost analysis presumably was to be one basis, although this analysis had been conducted under governmental pressure. The UGC had expanded its committee structure. The technology subcommittee had been reconstituted; new subcommittees on Latin American studies and on town and country planning had been established; and a joint panel on business schools and a committee on audio-visual aids in higher scientific education had been set up in cooperation with other agencies. Other so-called subject committees had also been established for the purpose, presumably, of avoiding unnecessary duplication in specialized departments and courses among the universities, and of allocating new subjects or specialities to selected institutions. These are certainly *limited* actions in the direction of planning and coordination, and I could only conclude that there was still little recognition of the necessity for planning a university system on a long-range scale and little conception of the range and depth of investigations necessary for producing a master plan for university development.

The Universal Problem of Public Accountability

It is interesting to note how comparable problems of planning, coordination, governmental influence, and public accountability arise at the same stages of university development in different countries. All these problems are matters of debate in the province of Ontario, Canada, where they became the subject of the Frank Gerstein Lectures at York University, Toronto, in 1966.

The government of Ontario made grants to no fewer than sixteen universities in 1964-65 in the amount of $101 million. It is pertinent, and I should think mandatory, to ask whether these grants were useful in particular institutions but essentially fortuitous with respect to the development of a comprehensive, differentiated, and coordinated system of higher education for the province.

In a paper on "The Evolution of a Provincial System of Higher Education in Ontario," Professor Robin S. Harris pointed out that "a provincial system of higher education involves more than the existence of a number of independent universities performing similar or related functions in response to a provincial demand. There must also be direction, coordination, and control."

How and by whom this direction, coordination, and control should be exercised is the subject of active consideration.

The provincial universities deal with the government through a Minister of University Affairs. Following British precedent, no doubt, a "buffer committee" has been appointed to provide independent advice to the universities, on the one hand, and the ministry on the other, and to provide a means of independent liaison between the government and the institutions.

As described by President Ross of York University, this is a body "made up of able citizens [the members are all laymen, no academics are included] who donate their time to the work of the committee, but all of whom have many other commitments. The committee has taken an interest in many matters other than budgets. For example, it took the initiative in calling for a study of graduate work in Ontario universities; it is interested in a general policy for student financial aid in the province; it is concerned about the development of new professional faculties and schools; and it is interested in many other broad issues of higher education. It has, however, tended to deal with individual problems rather than with a comprehensive and detached study of the whole—of which these individual problems, of course, are a part."[22]

President Ross has also asked the types of questions which an adequately organized and staffed planning and coordinating committee should be able to answer:

> Are these individual plans adequate for the demands of the future? Are the plans feasible? Do they overlap? Are there means by which some universities can specialize to avoid expensive duplication? Are there services . . . that can be centralized? Are the various graduate programs, professional faculties, areas of specialized study, related to each other and to the manpower needs of the future? Are all the universities in Ontario to be equal? . . . Can there be a master plan for higher education in Ontario?

It is apparent that the present Ontario Advisory Committee on University Affairs, as now organized, is far less capable than the University Grants Committee in Great Britain of planning the future development of higher education. Nevertheless, in his recent Gerstein Lecture, the Minister of University Affairs in Ontario put the matter squarely before the institutions when he said:

> . . . if they cannot or will not accept those responsibilities and if, for example, large numbers of able students must be turned away because the university is not prepared to accept them or if, as another example, some of the less glamorous disciplines are ignored, despite pressing demands for graduates in those areas, or if costly duplication of effort is evident, I cannot imagine that any society, especially one bearing large expense for higher edu-

cation, will want to stand idly by. For there will inevitably be a demand, and there have been indications of this in other jurisdictions, that government move in and take over . . . . I have already stressed that I am, as much as anyone, in favor of free and independent universities, for to my mind, they will serve our best interest. But this belief will not take away the question as to whether our institutions of higher learning can meet the challenge. Only our universities will be able to answer that.[23]

America: State-wide Coordination, an Attempted Answer

State-wide coordination of higher education has developed rapidly in the United States during the last two decades, but there is as yet little evidence on the effectiveness of various types of coordinating agencies and coordinating processes. Paltridge has pointed out that the number of states with some form of coordinating agency has increased from seventeen to forty-one since 1940. During this period there have been significant changes in the structure, organization, and powers of coordinating bodies. First, there is a tendency for agencies created by statute to replace purely voluntary coordinating bodies, such as the Council of State University Presidents in Michigan, which, it is not unfair to say, were often established primarily as a means of heading off threatened statutory mandates to curb wasteful competitive practices. Second, purely voluntary methods of coordination which may have been useful at an early stage in the development of a state's system of higher education, but which proved to be ineffective to deal with more complicated problems, are being superseded by coordinating bodies with statutory status and authority.[24]

These statutory boards take two principal forms. One type has advisory powers only and is composed primarily of members representing institutions and governing boards, although there is now a tendency, as in the case of the Coordinating Council in California, to add or increase lay membership on these bodies.

The second type of coordinating agency is given greater or lesser degrees of authority over such institutional affairs as educational programs, budgets, admission standards, and tuition. Examples of such agencies are the Board of Higher Education in Illinois and the Ohio Board of Regents for Higher Education, which have the power to approve all new educational programs—meaning any new unit of instruction, research, or public service, such as a college, school, division, institute, department, branch, or campus, and which are required to make recommendations to state executive and legislative bodies concerning operating and capital budgets.

Ohio and Illinois have coordinating boards which, in my mind, possess the minimally necessary powers. But such powers apparently do not guarantee productive institutional cooperation. Major state universities often resist coordination by super-boards, and so-called lesser state colleges and universities still struggle to take on the form, if not the substance, of the more prestigious universities. In 1959 the Center for the Study of Higher Education at Berkeley published the first large-scale study of state-wide coordination under the authorship of Lyman A. Glenny, now the Executive Officer of the Board of Higher Education in Illinois.[25]

It is now time for a second comprehensive investigation of the main problems in the development of higher education in the several states, the effectiveness of present means of planning and coordination, and more effective methods of promoting desirable educational development. After pointing out that "we seem to be plunging into all sorts of new arrangements without having asked and answered important prior questions," Logan Wilson has asked some of the questions that need to be answered. Among the questions he put were these:

> First, within a state, a region, or the nation, what kinds of decisions are best made by centralized authority and what kinds by localized authority? . . . How much of our traditional pluralism in higher education must we discard to become more efficient and effective? . . . Will the federal government's increased use of state agencies for the disbursement of educational support tend to promote centralization of authority or decentralization of authority? . . . Will the states' increasing use of state-wide governing or coordinating bodies result in a more rational approach to the growing problems of support and control? . . . Does it tend to politicize what ought to be professional decisions?[26]

Still another question that needs to be asked, as we have been reminded in this conference, is: What effect does placing a coordinating body between the state government and the governing boards of individual institutions or systems have on the relations of higher education to the state, and what influence does it have on the fundamental responsibility and accountability of institutions and governing boards? A final question for the moment: What is the effect of coordination, by whomever exercised, on educational experimentation and innovation?

The American Council on Education and the Center for Research and Development in Higher Education at Berkeley propose to study these and other questions.

The Universities Have Taken Over Government

Problems of state-wide planning and coordination are intricate enough, but new implications are on the horizon in the United States and elsewhere. To the north, the Canadian National Government now plays a minor role in financing provincial institutions, but its contribution is certain to grow, and ultimately it will assert a national interest in higher education. In the United States the federal interest has become a matter of far-reaching influence in the expansion of educational opportunity, the education of specialized personnel, the prosecution of basic and applied research, and the provision of educational facilities. The President and the Congress look upon colleges and universities as instruments of national power, as prime contributors to economic growth, as suppliers of specialists for government service, and as promoters of human welfare. Perhaps speaking too enthusiastically, Lord Bowden, head of the University of Manchester Institute of Science and Technology and erstwhile Minister of Science and Higher Education in the Wilson Government, wrote as follows about the interpenetration of society and the universities in the United States:

> You may say that the government has taken over the American universities. In a sense this is true; at the same time the universities have taken over the central government, and the whole nature and structure of American government has been transformed. Dons are everywhere in Washington—they run the science policy committees, they advise the President himself and most of his department heads.

> They have in the process produced a new type of society, a new machinery of government unlike anything I have seen anywhere else. The universities themselves are an essential component of this new machine. The system depends on free and frequent interchange of staff between the government, business, and the academic world . . . . There was once a time when scientists were content to live within the walls of their own laboratories; today they play a vitally important role in the formulation and execution of the national policy of every great nation.[27]

What may be said of the relationship of universities and the national government may also be said of the growing interdependence of education and industry, which supports university research and employs faculty members as consultants in science, technology, and management.

The price of this two-way street between universities on the one hand, and government and industry on the other, cannot yet be assessed with any accuracy. However, in this interchange the universities have almost certainly lost some of their prerogative to criticize, some of their freedom to speak out on controversial political and economic issues. President Clark Kerr of the University of California, as did President Eisenhower when he left office, warned that the alliance between industry and the Department of Defense might exert excessive influence on national policy. President Kerr might also have warned of the possible dangers to the integrity of the university from the *military-industrial-university* complex. How truly free is the University of California, which in 1964-65 obtained about $375 million, including $235 million for Atomic Energy Commission installations, from the federal government for research, teaching, building construction, and other purposes, and which in the process received millions of dollars in overhead allowances?

Interference by the Federal Government

I do not know of many overt instances (and the subtle ones are likely to be more significant) of interference by the federal government here, but I can give you two affecting the Research and Development Center in Higher Education. Until recently, the center was asked to file with the Office of Education, for its *information,* copies of all questionnaires, tests, or inventories used in investigations supported by funds from the Office of Education. Now, however, the center must submit such instruments (except intelligence and achievement tests) for *approval* in accordance with the Federal Reports Act of 1942, and the Office of Education has already censored certain items (and has tried to be helpful by suggesting revisions) in the Omnibus Personality Inventory, which was developed over a period of years in connection with the investigations of the Research and Development Center in Higher Education. It is ironic that the Omnibus Personality Inventory was developed primarily under subventions from the Carnegie Corporation of New York during the period when the present Secretary of Health, Education, and Welfare was president of that corporation. A second example of intervention is that the Office of Education reserves the right to approve the person appointed as Director of the Research and Development Center. Such controls seem to me to raise basic questions concerning the acceptability of federal support. Fortunately, the center is not entirely dependent on federal funds for its operation. Multiple sources of support, both public and private, are, I am convinced, essential to maintain freedom of investigation and independence from excessive external pressures and controls.

I shall take time for only one more example of impending and undesirable federal intervention. *Higher Education and National Affairs* for June 23, 1966,[28] stated that "efforts to avoid an imbalance between teaching and research in the administration of federal research programs will be instituted by the Bureau of the Budget, as the result of recommendations by the House Research and Technical Programs Subcommittee." The balance between teaching and research is a continuing university problem, and there is no question about the fact that the availability of large federal research grants and contracts has led some universities to expand research at the expense of both undergraduate and graduate instruction. But, I submit, this is a problem for the universities to control, not for the federal government to regulate. In one breath the Director of the Bureau of the Budget stated:

> It is primarily the responsibility of university administrators to apply restraints on the non-teaching activities of their professional staffs.

But in another breath he declared:

> Only in unusual and very limited circumstances should federal research support be provided in a form or amount such as to preclude any teaching by those engaged in research. While I believe this is a responsibility that must be shared by the agencies and the institutions, it would seem appropriate for the federal government to act on its own behalf to correct any imbalances that may be occurring.

Some of the dangers of allying the university with government and industry are obvious. Others are subtle. I believe that a careful study would show that, increasingly, the values of the academic man have become the values of the market place or the governmental arena and not the values of the free intellect. The age of faculty and university affluence has exalted economic advantage at the expense of human and humane values and to the detriment of the true university spirit.

Manna from Washington and Tomorrow's Tensions

Whatever the dangers of greater interdependence between higher education and the federal government may be, it is growing apace. "The first great federal impact on higher education," President Kerr pointed out recently, "came a century ago with encouragement of the land-grant universities, a movement which dramatically changed all universities, private and public, in the United States."[29] The vast grants for research from the Defense Department, the National Science Foundation, the National Institutes of Health, the National Aeronautics and Space Administration, and now the Office of Education, have had a profound effect, not wholly favorable, on research and teaching and on the balance of studies in the nation's major universities and even in some of the smaller liberal arts colleges, and on the traditional division between public and private higher education. In 1963-64, approximately one-fourth of the current fund income of public institutions came from the federal government—four-fifths of it for research. Even more— a third—of the current income of private universities came from federal sources. I have seen a statement that 80 percent of the budget of one private university comes from federal sources. This institution may still be formally controlled by its board of trustees, but it is obviously in many ways at the mercy of the government.

The Higher Education Act of 1965 authorized about $2.5 billion over three years for a wide range of programs—community service, library materials and research, aid for developing colleges, educational opportunity grants for undergraduates, guaranteed reduced-interest loans for undergraduates and graduates, expansion of work-study, a National Teachers Corps, fellowships for teachers, laboratory and instructional equipment, and undergraduate and graduate educational facilities. This was only a part of the manna from Washington—there were additional grants for teaching, research, and facilities in the health sciences, for example. It has been estimated that next year the federal government's involvement, directly and indirectly, for research and other purposes in colleges and universities will reach $4 billion.[30]

With all this goes talk about a nationwide (which may not be synonymous with federal) policy for higher education—although few concrete proposals have been adduced concerning how such a policy should be developed out of a congeries of voluntary and statutory educational organizations.[31]

Large-scale federal assistance is certain to have a profound impact on the relationships among educational institutions. This support will greatly affect not only the total resources available in a given state for higher education, but also the method of their allocation. It will also influence the roles which particular institutions may be expected to play in a state-wide system, or in a region; the quality of education throughout the system; the development of graduate, professional, and post-doctoral educational programs; the access of students to different institutions and different levels of education; the mobility of students within the system, as well as among the states; greater centralization of authority at both state and federal levels; and a host of other consequences.

By selecting the recipients of federal largess, the government has already exercised a considerable degree of coordination, and it will bring about still more at national, regional, and state levels. There is no time here to recount the methods already applied or to explore future means of attaining concerted effort. Suffice it to say that the relations of the universities and the government have taken on a new dimension.

We may expect to see the tension between institutional independence and public accountability grow in intensity. There will be greater stress between the desire for autonomy and the pressure for coordinated effort. It will take all the statesmanship the academic community and the government together can muster to enable colleges and universities to serve the broader public interest while preserving the identity, integrity, initiative, and morale of individual institutions and, especially, the intellectual freedom of faculty and students.

[1]L. A. Cremin, *The Genius of American Education*. Pittsburgh: The University of Pittsburgh Press, 1965, pp. 95-96.

[2]P. F. Lazarsfeld and Thielens, Wagner, Jr., *The Academic Mind*. Glencoe, Illinois: The Free Press, 1958, pp. 176, 178-179.

[3]Quoted in American Council on Education, *Higher Education and National Affairs*, Vol. 15, No. 21, Jan. 23, 1966.

[4]University of Oxford, *Report of Commission of Inquiry*. Volume I. Oxford: Oxford University Press, 1966.

[5]Committee on Government and Higher Education, *The Efficiency of Freedom*. Baltimore: The Johns Hopkins Press, 1959, p. 9.

[6]*Ibid.*, p. 12.

[7]Staff Report for the Coordinating Council for Higher Education, *Recognition of Fiscal Authority and Responsibility for the Trustees of the California State Colleges*. March 29, 1966.

[8]Committee on Government and Higher Education, *op. cit.*, pp. 14-15.

[9]C. K. Arnold, "Higher Education: Fourth Branch of Government?" *Saturday Review*, Jan. 18, 1964.

[10]Sir Eric Ashby, "Some Problems of Universities in New Countries of the British Commonwealth." *Comparative Education* 2:1-10, Nov. 1965.

[11]Murray G. Ross, "The President's Report," *These Five Years*. Toronto, Canada, York University, 1965.

[12]Sir Eric Ashby, *op. cit.*

[13]Sir Eric Ashby, "The University Ideal." Address at the convocation on "The University in America," Center for the Study of Democratic Institutions, Los Angeles, May 9, 1966 (mimeographed).

[14]J. L. Morrill, *The Ongoing State University*. Minneapolis: University of Minnesota Press, 1960, p. 103.

[15]T. R. McConnell, *A General Pattern for American Public Higher Education*. New York: McGraw-Hill, 1962, p. 109.

[16]Sir Eric Ashby, "The University Ideal", *op. cit.*

[17]Sir Eric Ashby, "Some Problems of Universities in New Countries of the British Commonwealth," *op. cit.*

[18]London, Her Majesty's Stationery Office, May, 1966.

[19]Marjorie Reeves, "Prestige," in Marjorie Reeves (Editor), *Eighteen Plus: Unity and Diversity in Higher Education*. London: Faber and Faber, Ltd., 1965, pp. 151-154.

[20]Sir Peter Venables, "Confusion, Concentration and Clarification in Higher Education," *Comparative Education* 2:11-18, Nov., 1965. Lord Robbins has also objected to the proposed binary system on the same grounds. See Lord Robbins and Boris Ford, "Report on Robbins," *Universities Quarterly* 20:5-15, Dec., 1965.

[21]T. R. McConnell, "The Coordination of State Systems of Higher Education" in Logan Wilson (ed.), *Emerging Patterns in American Higher Education*, Washington, D.C.: American Council on Education, 1965, p. 130.

[22]Murray G. Ross, *op. cit.*

[23]W. G. Davis, "The Government of Ontario and the Universities of the Province." Frank Gerstein Lecture, 1966, York University, Toronto (mimeographed).

[24]James G. Paltridge, "Organizational Forms which Characterize Statewide Coordination of Public Higher Education." Unpublished paper (mimeographed).

[25]L. A. Glenny, *Autonomy of Public Colleges: The Challenge of Coordination*. New York: McGraw-Hill, 1959.

[26]Logan Wilson, "Diversity and Divisiveness in Higher Education," pp. 5-8 in *Selected Papers*. Forty-sixth Annual Convention, American Association of Junior Colleges. Washington, The Association, 1966.

[27]Lord Bowden, "The Place of Universities in Modern Society." *Comparative Education* 1:45-62, March, 1965.

[28]Washington: American Council on Education.

[29]Clark Kerr, "Toward a Nationwide System of Higher Education," in Logan Wilson (ed.), *op. cit.*, pp. 258-271.

[30]K. Spaulding, "The Relevance of Federal Programs to the Purpose of the Institution." *Educational Record* 47:139-147, Spring, 1966.

[31]See, for example, Kerr, Clark, *op cit.*; and Wilson, Logan, "Basic Premises for a National Policy in Higher Education" in Logan Wilson (ed.), *op. cit.*, pp. 263-271.

See Section VII in the back of this book

for annotated bibliography of related materials.

BIBLIOGRAPHY

Section I

The University and State Government: Fears and Realities

Allen, H. K. *Finance and State Institutions of Higher Education in the United States*. New York: Columbia University Press, 1952. 181 pp.

Written directly after W.W. II influx in our higher education enrollment, the book is concerned with new ways for states to obtain the necessary revenue to maintain their educational systems. After analyzing present state tax structures the only hope is seen in establishing a broad based retail sales tax and a moderately progressive income tax.

Blackwell, Thomas E. *College Law: A Guide for Administrators*. Washington, D. C.: American Council on Education, 1961. 347 pp.

Although the book covers an extensive amount of material, chapters VII and VIII are of primary importance. Blackwell is able to put many of the questions such as "Is education a function of government?" and "Are some state universities constitutionally independent corporations?" into a concise, logical perspective. His discussion of certain state officials' interference with the internal administration of institutions of higher education, i.e., state administration agencies, state auditors, and state treasurers, is very illuminating.

——————. "Legislative Control of Tax Supported Universities," *College and University Business*, Vol. XXVI (September, 1956), pp. 34-35.

The author argues that the majority of state supported colleges and universities are now considered to be public corporations created by the state legislature and subject to their control.

Browne, Arthur D. "The Institution and the System: Autonomy and Coordination," *Long-Range Planning in Higher Education*, Owen A. Knorr, Ed. Boulder, Colo.: The Western Interstate Commission for Higher Education, 1964, pp. 39-51.

The case of autonomy versus coordination as applied to long-range planning is presented. The evidence points to a split decision, with each a winner if it is willing to pay a price. But the cost of winning is high, for it involves restraint and sacrifice, which means the subjugation of personal interests to the welfare of the total educational enterprise.

Brumbaugh, A. J. "Proper Relationships Between State Government and State-Supported Higher Institutions," *Educational Record,* Vol. 42, No. 3 (July, 1961), pp. 173-178.

Forces encroaching on institutional autonomy are identified. The factors contributing to the trend toward external controls of state colleges and universities are discussed. The author offers five conclusions concerning the relationships between the state and its institutions of higher education.

——————. *State-Wide Planning and Coordination of Higher Education.* Atlanta, Georgia: Southern Regional Education Board, 1963. 45 pp.

This book represents a concise and short summary of the requirements for an effective state-wide planning and coordination agency. Several states are used as guidelines in describing the operation and functions of state planning boards. The author feels such an independent agency is needed in order to bring together the common objectives of both the citizens and the institutions of higher learning.

Campbell, Roald F. and Gerald R. Sroufe. "Toward a Rationale for Federal-State-Local Relations in Education," *Phi Delta Kappan,* Vol. XLVII, No. 1 (September, 1965), pp. 2-7.

The increasing activity of the federal government in education demands examination and if possible the development of a rationale which would suggest the nature of an appropriate partnership among federal, state, and local governments as they relate to education. The thesis follows: (1) the present situation is confused; (2) ours was a national federalism from the beginning; (3) there has been a gradual shift toward increased national federalism; (4) national federalism is a basis for viewing recent policy developments in higher education; and (5) a rationale for policy-sharing among national, state, and local governments is needed.

Chambers, M. M. *Freedom and Repression in Higher Education.* Bloomington, Indiana: The Bloomcraft Press, Inc., 1965. 126 pp.

In the author's words he has "struggled to explain and present favorably the principle of individual freedom of choice and of institutional autonomy in higher education . . ." which to him are more important than centralized planning and administrative bureaucracy. Dr. Conant's book, *Shaping Educational Policy,* is heavily criticized on the grounds that Chambers feels diversity rather than unity ". . . is needed in a state's higher education policy and at all costs our systems of higher education should steer away from any uniformity or regimentation of a bureaucratic nature."

——————. *Voluntary Statewide Coordination in Public Higher Education.* Ann Arbor, Michigan: The University of Michigan, 1961. 80 pp.

The author continues his theme of non-compulsory planning and administering of state higher education in the hands of a formal agency. He asks some pointed questions as to the real benefit such organizations actually provide. He feels that "neither at the state level nor the national level do Americans want a rigidly structured 'European ministry of education' type of control of public colleges and universities." He analyzes in separate chapters the systems of higher education in California, Colorado, Indiana, Ohio, and Michigan.

The Committee on Government and Higher Education. *The Efficiency of Freedom.* Baltimore, Md.: Johns Hopkins Press, 1959. 44 pp.

This study, financed by The Fund for the Advancement of Education, has as its objectives: (1)to define the relationships that should properly exist between public officials and state institutions of higher education; (2) to identify the principal areas in which state control over higher education has appeared to exceed proper limits and thus to lead to unwarranted political or bureaucratic intrusion into educational policy or effective educational administration; and (3) to suggest basic remedial lines of action.

Coons, Arthur G. and others. *A Master Plan for Higher Education in California, 1960-1975.* Sacramento, Calif.: California State Department of Education, 1960. 230 pp.

This volume, as prepared for the Liaison Committee of the Regents of the University of California and the California State Board of Education, forms a comprehensive analysis and projection of the state needs in higher education for a fifteen-year period. Includes index, tables, and appendices.

Coordinating Two-Year Colleges in State Education Systems. A Report of a Conference in Washington, D. C., May 16-17, 1957. U. S. Department of Health, Education, and Welfare, Office of Education. Washington: Government Printing Office, 1957.

The role of the state directors and supervisors of two-year colleges in coordinating these institutions in a state educational system is identified. Brief descriptions are included of the organization and scheme for operation and control of two-year institutions in sixteen states.

DeZonia, Robert H. "Coordination Among Higher Institutions in Wisconsin," *Educational Record,* Vol. 44, No. 3 (July, 1963), pp. 288-293.

The author presents a brief overview and analysis of the coordinating committee for higher education in Wisconsin. Although the committee has created certain frictions within the state, the author feels that it has contributed significantly to the advancement of higher education.

"Freedom Crusade of the University of Massachusetts," *Educational Record,* Vol. XXXVIII (April, 1957), pp. 100-111.

An account, through the use of documents and press clippings, of how the university regained control of its personnel policies through a hard-fought campaign for public support led by the president. Offers a good look at a case study on how university officials can maintain local autonomy and control of university policies.

Glenny, Lyman A. *Autonomy of Public Colleges*. New York: McGraw-Hill, 1959. 325 pp.

The author in this work presents a comprehensive description of the existing patterns of coordination in higher education within states until 1957. Through a process of extensive personal interviewing of governors, college presidents, legislators, and state and university administrative officers, the author is able to present a picture of the various coordinating agencies and boards throughout the United States. The book therefore attempts to enable legislators and educators to have a better understanding of what type of coordinating relationship within their state can best achieve a higher quality of higher education while not sacrificing such concepts as autonomy and freedom.

—————————. "State Systems and Plans for Higher Education," *Emerging Patterns in American Higher Education,* Logan Wilson, Ed. Washington, D. C.: American Council on Education, 1965. pp. 86-103.

"Diversity continues to be cherished and encouraged by all, but today the unlimited freedom of a college or university to pursue a self-determined destiny is rapidly being curtailed among the public institutions and even has prospects of diminishing among the non-public ones. At the state level the new watchwords are cooperation and coordination, with institutional autonomy only within certain new perimeters. The classic condition of autonomy in higher education still prevails in only ten states . . . ."

Green, Ralph T. "The Need for Coordination and Controls in the Financing of State Institutions," *Proceedings of the 55th Annual Conference of the National Tax Association, 1962.* Harrisburg, Pa.: National Tax Association, 1963, pp. 476-82.

The author suggests that financial requests for institutions of higher education be handled and controlled through a coordinating board which then presents recommendations to the legislature. He contends that the legislative committees have neither the time nor ability to handle the volumes of factual material that support requests, and are unable to truly differentiate between institutions.

Harris, Seymour E. *Challenge and Change in American Education.* Berkeley, Calif.: McCutchan Publishing Corporation, 1965. 346 pp.

Second in a series of three books edited by Seymour Harris based on the Seminars in American Education at Harvard University between 1958-1963. Three broad topics are presented: "Government and Education"; "Challenges in Educational Planning"; "Management."

—————. *More Resources for Education*: The John Dewey Society Annual Lecture, February 12, 1960. New York: Harper and Bros., 1960. 85 pp.

It is shown that expenditures in all levels of education have not kept pace with the use in other levels of expenditures by all levels of our government. Higher education is by far the more complex problem in education than lower and will require more than just additional money. New mechanisms of finance as well as a redistribution of emphasis from local support to federal must come about in order to alleviate the tremendous burden placed on local and state governments.

Henderson, Algo. "The Role of the State in Higher Education," *Educational Record*, Vol. XXXII (January, 1951), pp. 64-69.

The author identifies four functions of the state in the field of higher education: (1) assures for youth equality of opportunity in education; (2) fosters the development of the resources of a country, with higher education as a means of developing the human resources; (3) assures the facilities in higher education are significant to meet the needs and that the programs are of adequate quality; and (4) stimulates research and supports research programs of its own.

Hill, W. W., Jr. "State Supported Student Loan Programs," *Proceedings, 55th Annual Conference of the National Tax Association, 1962*. Harrisburg, Pa.: National Tax Association, 1963. pp. 493-501.

Author indicates that soon, 25 percent of all college students may be borrowing money for college expenses and up to 10 percent of all college expenses may be met by loans. A director of one of the nation's largest private college loan companies, he urges local, state, and voluntary efforts in the area and argues against government involvement on a massive scale.

Horner, Harlan E. "The State and Higher Education," *University of the State of New York Bulletin*. Albany, New York: The University of the State of New York, April 15, 1939. pp. 5-35.

Illinois Board of Higher Education. *A Master Plan for Higher Education in Illinois*. Springfield, Illinois: Board of Higher Education, July, 1964. 72 pp.

The plan is a comprehensive study of educational needs in public and non-public colleges and universities and other educational enterprises. It looks at questions such as how should public colleges and universities be governed? What structure is to be provided for the most economical operation? To what extent is unified planning and coordination useful? To what extent should non-public institutions be involved in state-wide planning? Chapter 6 on financing and chapter 7 on organization and coordination are of special worth.

Martorana, S. V. and Ernest V. Hollis. *State Boards Responsible for Higher Education*. Office of Education, U. S. Department of Health, Education, and Welfare, Circular No. 619. Washington: Government Printing Office, 1960. 254 pp.

Although dated, this volume is still an important study in the coordination of institutions of higher education. It is organized with a broad overview, analysis, and evaluation of state boards; a state-by-state analysis of the organization of public higher education in the United States; and a number of basic reference tables pertaining to state organization. Includes an appendix on the "Allocation of Operating Funds by Boards for Higher Education" authored by A. J. Brumbaugh and Myron R. Blee.

McConnell, T. R. "The Coordination of State Systems of Higher Education," *Emerging Patterns in American Higher Education,* Logan Wilson, Ed. Washington, D. C.: American Council on Education, 1965, pp. 129-141.

The author gives comprehensive coverage to the development and forms of the various state systems of coordination and cooperation in higher education. Areas covered include: Voluntary Systems; The Single Board; The Coordinating Board; Coordinated Planning; and Major Trends in Coordination. Includes select bibliography.

——————. *A Restudy of the Needs of California in Higher Education.* Sacramento, Calif.: California State Department of Education, 1955. 473 pp.

As prepared for the Liaison Committee of the Regents of the University of California and the California State Board of Education, this volume supplemented and replaced the original study of the needs of higher education in the state completed in 1948. Included in this extensive state study are: The Needs for Higher Education in California, as measured by the population to be served; The Functions and Programs of Higher Education in California; The Government, Administration, and Coordination of Public Higher Education; The Present Physical Plants and Future Plants Needed; and California's Ability to Support Higher Education.

Miller, James L., Jr. "The Two Dimensions of State-Wide Higher Education Coordination," *Educational Record,* Vol. 43, No. 2 (April, 1962), pp. 163-167.

The author briefly describes different types of state coordination and coordinating bodies, but the primary concern is with the dimensions of coordination. The first is geographic coordination termed horizontal due to its concern for providing equal educational opportunities across a state; the second is program coordination termed vertical because it concerns itself with research and the pyramid of educational programs. Although effective coordination is not assured by a formal state organization, the author believes that more and more states are going to adopt some form of formal organization in the future.

Millet, J. D. "State Planning for Higher Education," *Educational Record,* Vol. 46, No. 3 (Summer, 1965), pp. 223-30.

Millet, a professor of public administration, aptly deals with the topic of state planning which he feels must be established so that in the political process of taxation, borrowing, and spending higher education planning can present its needs comprehensively and justify its objectives reasonably. Relationship of planning agency and the institution along with the context of a state master plan are discussed.

Moos, Malcolm and Frances E. Rourke. *The Campus and the State*. Baltimore, Md.: The Johns Hopkins Press, 1959. 414 pp.

A study of the challenge and response in the day-to-day relationships between public institutions of higher education and American state governments. The authors believe that the trend toward administrative centralization within the states has been a major factor in introducing greater stress into relations between public colleges and universities and state government.

Morey, Lloyd. "Governmental Control of Public Higher Education," *Transactions and Proceedings of the National Association of State Universities,* Vol. LIII (1955), pp. 30-41.

The author maintains that a state institution of higher education, as a part of the state, and receiving its main support from the state, should and does have responsibility and accountability to the government and, through it, to the public.

Morrison, D. G. and S. V. Martorana. *Criteria for the Establishment of Two-Year Colleges*. Office of Education, United States Department of Health, Education, and Welfare. Washington: Government Printing Office, 1962. 70 pp.

Examines the various formulas and patterns of support for two-year colleges and reviews the proportion of this support which is received from the state, from the district, and from student sources. Six questions relating to financing the two-year colleges are posed with brief comments.

Mushkin, Selma J. and Eugene P. McLoone. *Public Spending for Higher Education in 1970*. Chicago, Ill.: Council of State Governments, February, 1965. 68 pp.

As part of Project '70', a series of studies of state revenues and expenditures projected to 1970, this publication is concerned with questions raised if higher education needs are to be met in 1970. Contending that this probably is the fastest growing area of state expenditures during the coming five years, the authors look at present figures and, assuming certain economic and demographic conditions, project the necessities of 1970, and the amount of additional tax support required. Includes appendices showing statistics on a state-by-state breakdown.

—————. "State Financing of Higher Education," *Economics of Higher Education*. Office of Education, United States Department of Health, Education, and Welfare. Washington: Government Printing Office, 1962, pp. 218-249.

A comprehensive review of the ways and means state governments are using to meet their threefold responsibilities for higher education: (1) to answer educational opportunities for growing number of qualified students; (2) to develop manpower capabilities in numbers adequate to supply vital public services; and (3) to build higher educational potential so necessary to economic progress in the state.

Nevins, Allan. *The State University and Democracy*. Urbana, Illinois: University of Illinois Press, 1962. 171 pp.

An historical work on the four stages of development in our state and land-grant institutions, with special attention to their contributions to democracy. Current trends in enrollment, academic curriculum, and structure of public and private institutions. Of special note is chapter 4 on future trends.

Pierce, Truman M. *Federal, State and Local Government in Education*. Washington, D. C.: Center for Applied Research in Education, 1964. 120 pp.

Viewpoint throughout the book is that education under the auspices of government has both reflected and strengthened concepts of individual freedom and opportunity. Issues such as control, goals, financing, and church and state are each discussed in regard to the role each branch of government will play in determining these issues. Bibliography, pp. 113-114.

Reeves, H. C. "Higher Education and State Tax Policy," *National Tax Journal,* Vol. 291 (1962), pp. 291-296.

Starting with the premise that responsibility for providing a basic program of higher education lies with the state, the author proposes that states should allow tax credits for general purpose contributions to private colleges and universities. The state corporation income tax is suggested as the best vehicle to implement this kind of policy and would provide those in high income brackets with an attractive alternative to other donations. The proposal voices a genuine concern for the maintaining of voluntary support for private higher education.

Reports on Higher Education. An Annotated Bibliography of Recent Reports of State Study Commissions and Other Official Agencies. Chicago, Ill.: The Council of State Governments, March, 1958. 15 pp. (Mimeographed)

An annotated bibliography of seventeen official state reports on higher education. The annotations include the major subjects covered in each report and a summary of the recommendations.

Sliger, B. F. and Thomas R. Beard. "State Support of Public Higher Education," *Proceedings, 55th Annual Conference of the National Tax Association, 1962*. Harrisburg, Pa.: National Tax Association, 1963, pp. 464-76.

In answering the questions (1) how much should be spent on higher education, and (2) how much of the responsibility will fall upon state-supported—as opposed to private institutions of higher learning, the authors discuss state support in terms of: Higher Education and Optimum Resource Allocation; Needs and Means of State-Supported Higher Education; The Role of the States in Public Higher Education; and State Support vs. Higher Tuitions.

Smylie, R. E. "Legislative Workshops—A Method of Improving Communication with Higher Education," *State Government,* Vol. 32 (1959), pp. 266-271.

Governor Smylie of Idaho, in this speech given to the Western Governors' Conference in 1959, ably expresses the need for legislators, state officials, and educators of their regions to jointly examine the needs of higher education. His analysis of the western states' problems in higher education are accurate and concise. Smylie specifically describes the contrasting motives and concerns of legislators and educators.

Strand, A. L. "Land-Grant Colleges and the State," *Proceedings of the Association of Land-Grant Colleges and Universities,* Vol. 67 (1953), pp. 221-225.

Report of a survey of 47 land-grant colleges from 46 states and one territory identifying the controls over the colleges which become operative after the legislative appropriations to the institutions have been made.

The University of the State of New York, State Education Department. *The Regents' State-wide Plan for the Expansion and Development of Higher Education, 1964.* Albany, N. Y.: The University of the State of New York Press, April, 1965. 131 pp.

Every four years the State Board of Regents must submit a comprehensive plan for the orderly development of higher education. This is their first plan. The report is an extensive document covering every aspect of education and the peculiar organization and relationship of New York public and private schools. Report deals at length with the state needs—both the state and the society. Part IV deals with the institution plans and the means of the master plan to achieve identity, unity, and excellence throughout the university.

"What About Services of State Departments of Education?" *Bulletin of the Bureau of School Services.* Lexington, Kentucky: College of Education, University of Kentucky, June, 1955.

Eight critical requirements, expressed in terms of abilities of staff members, are listed as influencing the effective performance of services.

Wilson, Logan, Ed. *Emerging Patterns in American Higher Education.* A collection of essays. Washington, D. C.: American Council on Education, 1965. 292 pp.

This volume of essays is contributed by the nation's leading educators and scholars; it is a comprehensive overview of American higher education today. Directed primarily at organization and direction, it covers: the changing environment of higher education; institutional modifications; the emergence of state systems; voluntary arrangements; interinstitutional and interstate agreements; unified approaches to national problems; national associations in higher education; and national policy for higher education: problems and prospects. Primary emphasis is toward the emergence of a stronger national higher educational policy.

Wooden, William P. "State Universities—Legislative Control of a Constitutional Corporation," *Michigan Law Review,* Vol. 55, No. 5 (March, 1957), pp. 728-730.

Article reviews the decision of the Utah Supreme Court on the issue of whether or not a university corporation is free from any control by the state. The court found that such a corporation, i.e., Michigan, California, and Colorado, is merely an independent province and, as such, legislative enactments will prevail over the rules and regulations made by the university where the matter in question is not an exclusively university affair . . . . Of special interest with regard to the influence of the state government to the campus is the legislative control of the university when "conditions are attached to university appropriations."

Some of the annotated listings in this section have been reproduced from *Selected Issues in Higher Education; An Annotated Bibliography* with the permission of Teachers College Press, Columbia University.

Section II

Maintaining Institutional Identity and Autonomy in Coordinated Systems

Axelrod, Joseph and others. *Autonomy and Interdependence: Emerging Systems in Higher Education.* Washington, D. C.: American Council on Education, 1964. 89 pp.

This volume is comprised of five resource papers written as background for discussions at the Annual Meeting of the American Council on Education in 1964. The five topics deal in general with the conflicting concepts in higher education of "autonomy" and "interdependence." Topics covered include: "New Organizational Patterns in American Colleges and Universities"; "Consortia and Related Interinstitutional Arrangements in Higher Education"; "Interstate Cooperation and Coordination in Higher Education"; "National Organizations in Higher Education."

Blackwell, Thomas E. *College Law: A Guide for Administrators.* Washington, D. C.: American Council on Education, 1961. 347 pp.

Although the book covers an extensive amount of material, chapters VII and VIII are of primary importance. Blackwell is able to put many of the questions such as "Is education a function of government?" and "Are some state universities constitutional independent corporations?" into a concise, logical perspective. His discussion of certain state officials' interference with the internal administration of institutions of higher education, i.e., state administration agencies, state auditors, and state treasurers, is very illuminating.

—————. "Legislative Control of Tax Supported Universities," *College and University Business,* Vol. XXVI (September, 1956), pp. 34-6.

The author argues that the majority of state-supported colleges and universities are now considered to be public corporations created by the state legislatures and subject to their control.

Browne, Arthur D. "The Institution and the System: Autonomy and Coordination," *Long-Range Planning in Higher Education,* Owen A. Knorr, Ed. Boulder, Colo.: The Western Interstate Commission for Higher Education, 1964. pp. 39-51.

The case of autonomy versus coordination as applied to long-range planning is presented. The evidence points to a split decision, with each a winner if it is willing to pay a price. But the cost of winning is high, for it involves restraint and sacrifice, which means the subjugation of personal interests to the welfare of the total educational enterprise.

Brumbaugh, A. J. "Proper Relationships Between State Government and State-supported Higher Institutions," *Educational Record,* Vol. 42, No. 3 (July, 1961), pp. 173-178.

Forces encroaching on institutional autonomy are identified. The factors contributing to the trend toward external controls of state colleges and universities are discussed. The author offers five conclusions concerning the relationships between the state and its institutions of higher education.

————. *State-wide Planning and Coordination of Higher Education.* Atlanta, Georgia: Southern Regional Education Board, 1963. 45 pp.

This book represents a concise and short summary of the requirements for an effective state-wide planning and coordination agency. Several states are used as guidelines in describing the operation and functions of state planning boards. The author feels such an independent agency is needed in order to bring together the common objectives of both the citizens and the institutions of higher learning.

Chambers, M. M. *Freedom and Repression in Higher Education.* Bloomington, Indiana: The Bloomcraft Press, Inc., 1965. 126 pp.

In the author's words, he has "struggled to explain and present favorably the principle of individual freedom of choice and of institutional autonomy in higher education . . ." which to him are more important than centralized planning and administrative bureaucracy. Dr. Conant's book, *Shaping Educational Policy,* is heavily criticized on the grounds that Chambers feels diversity rather than unity ". . . is needed in a state's higher education policy, and at all costs our systems of higher education should steer away from any uniformity or regimentation of a bureaucratic nature."

————. *Voluntary State-wide Coordination in Public Higher Education.* Ann Arbor, Michigan: The University of Michigan Press, 1961. 80 pp.

The author analyzes systems of non-compulsory planning and administering of state higher education in the hands of a formal agency. He asks some pointed questions as to the real benefit such organizations actually provide. He feels that "neither at the state level nor the national level do Americans want a rigidly structured 'European ministry of education' type of control of public colleges and universities." He analyzes in separate chapters the systems of higher education in California, Colorado, Indiana, Ohio, and Michigan.

The Committee on Government and Higher Education. *The Efficiency of Freedom.* Baltimore, Md.: Johns Hopkins Press, 1959. 44 pp.

This study, financed by the Fund for the Advancement of Education, has as its objectives: (1) to define the relationships that should properly exist between public officials and state institutions of higher education; (2) to identify the principal areas in which state control over higher education has appeared to exceed proper limits and thus to lead to unwarranted political or bureaucratic intrusion into educational policy or effective educational administration; and (3) to suggest basic remedial lines of action.

Evan, William M. "The Organization-Set: Toward a Theory of Interorganizational Relations," *Approaches to Organizational Development,* James D. Thompson, Ed. Pittsburgh, Pa.: University of Pittsburgh Press, 1966. pp. 173-91.

Social science research on organizations has been concerned principally with intraorganizational phenomena. The relative neglect of interorganizational relations is surprising in view of the fact that all formal organizations are embedded in an environment of other organizations as well as in a complex of norms, values, and collectivities of the society at large. The phenomena and problems of interorganizational relations are part of the general class of boundary-relations problems confronting all types of social systems, including formal organizations.

"Freedom Crusade of the University of Massachusetts," *Educational Record,* Vol. XXXVIII (April, 1957), pp. 100-111.

An account, through the use of documents and press clippings, of how the university regained control of its personal policies through a hard fought campaign for public support led by the president. Offers a good look at a case study on how university officials can maintain local autonomy and control of university policies.

Glenny, Lyman A. *Autonomy of Public Colleges.* New York: McGraw-Hill, 1959. 325 pp.

The author in this work presents a comprehensive description of the existing patterns of coordination in higher education within states until 1957. Through a process of extensive personal interviewing of governors, college presidents, legislators, and state and university administrative officers, the author is able to present a valuable picture of the various coordinating agencies and boards throughout the United States. The book therefore attempts to enable legislators and educators to have a better understanding of what type of coordinating relationship within their state can best achieve a higher quality of higher education while not sacrificing such concepts as autonomy and freedom.

——————. "State Systems and Plans for Higher Education," *Emerging Patterns in American Higher Education,* Logan Wilson, Ed. Washington, D. C.: American Council on Education, 1965. pp. 86-103.

"Diversity continues to be cherished and encouraged by all, but today the unlimited freedom of a college or university to pursue a self-determined destiny is rapidly being curtailed among the public institutions and even has prospects of diminishing among the non-public ones. At the state level the new watchwords are cooperation and coordination, with institutional autonomy only within certain parameters. The classic condition of autonomy in higher education still prevails in only ten states. . . ."

Kerr, Clark. *The Uses of the University*: Godkin Lectures. Cambridge, Mass.: Harvard University Press, 1963. 140 pp.

This contribution to higher education, written by the president of the conglomerate University of California, contains material on the actual effect of massive subsidies and a university's subsequent position when federal aid is given to it in any form. Of special interest is chapter 2 entitled "Federal Grant Universities."

Litwak, Eugene and Lydia F. Hylton. "Interorganizational Analysis: A Hypothesis on Coordinating Agencies," *Administrative Science Quarterly,* Vol. 6 (March, 1962), pp. 395-426.

A theory of interorganizational coordination is presented based upon: (1) organizational interdependence, (2) level of organizational awareness, (3) standardization of organizational activities, and (4) number of organizations. The authors indicate a theory of limited conflict as opposed to traditional harmony theory.

Millet, J. D. "State Planning for Higher Education," *Educational Record,* Vol. 46, No. 3 (Summer, 1965), pp. 223-30.

The impression is conveyed that state planning for higher education is no bed of roses. It is not a field for the timorous, the anxious, the sensitive. But it is a field where much can be accomplished if all involved in public higher education will work together with intelligence, good will, and a sense of compromise. The alternative is a return to a jungle political warfare in which reason is likely to play a small role and naked power will decide the issues.

Perkins, James A. "The New Conditions of Autonomy," *Emerging Patterns in American Higher Education,* Logan Wilson, Ed. Washington, D. C.: The American Council on Education, 1965. pp. 8-17.

Within the context of academic freedom and university autonomy, the author discusses the relationship between modern government, industry, and education and the combinations of interests. Specifically covered are: Growth and Specialization; Decentralization and Specialization; Faculty and Administration; State, Regional, and National Organizations; International Agencies; and The Hierarchy of Structures. He concludes that a large degree of autonomy is necessary if the university is to properly perform its function and maintain academic freedom and that this autonomy will depend primarily upon the statesmanship abilities of university administrators.

The University of the State of New York, State Education Department. *The Regents' State-wide Plan for the Expansion and Development of Higher Education, 1964*. Albany, N. Y.: The University of the State of New York Press, April, 1965. 131 pp.

Every four years the State Board of Regents must submit a comprehensive plan for the orderly development of higher education. This is their first plan. The report is an extensive document covering every aspect of education and the peculiar organization and relationship of New York public and private schools. Report deals at length with the state needs to both the state and the society. Part IV deals with the institution plans and the means of the master plan to achieve identity, unity, and excellence throughout the university.

Wilson, Logan, Ed. *Emerging Patterns in American Higher Education*. A collection of essays. Washington, D. C.: American Council on Education, 1965. 292 pp.

This volume of essays is contributed by the nation's leading educators and scholars; it is a comprehensive overview of American higher education today. Directed primarily at organization and direction, it covers: the changing environment of higher education; institutional modifications; the emergence of state systems; voluntary arrangements; interinstitutional and interstate agreements; unified approaches to national problems; national associations in higher education; and national policy for higher education: problems and prospects. Primary emphasis is toward the emergence of a stronger national higher educational policy.

——————. *Diversity and Divisiveness in Higher Education*. Unpublished speech delivered to the American Association of Junior Colleges, March 1, 1966.

"Our system of higher education was organized largely in discrete units, with local boards, administrators, and faculties exercising considerable autonomy in the determination of their own means and ends. But the growing importance, expense, and interdependence of higher education institutions are forces exerting heavy pressures to change all this. . . ."

——————. "Myths and Realities of Institutional Independence," *Emerging Patterns in American Higher Education,* Logan Wilson, Ed. Washington, D.C.: American Council on Education, 1965, pp. 18-28.

In this article the author addresses himself to the problem of what is a "proper" or "improper" constraint on an institution's independence. By tracing past traditions of institutional autonomy and present influences on this autonomy the author suggests that we can no longer reject the idea that our colleges and universities operate in a highly interdependent era which is becoming more "politicized" every year. In conclusion Wilson feels university organization and administration has lacked the concentrated reorganization and change which industry and government have long been experiencing.

Wooden, William P. "State Universities—Legislative Control of a Constitutional Corporation," *Michigan Law Review,* Vol. 55, No. 5 (March, 1957), pp. 728-730.

Article reviews the decision of the Utah Supreme Court on the issue of whether or not a university corporation is free from any control by the state. The court found that such a corporation, i.e., Michigan, California, and Colorado, is merely an independent province and, as such, legislative enactments will prevail over the rules and regulations made by the university where the matter in question is not an exclusively university affair. . . . Of special interest with regard to the influence of the state government to the campus is the legislative control of the university when "conditions are attached to university appropriations."

Section III

Politics and Current Patterns in Coordinating Higher Education

Allen, James E. "The Compact: New Strength for the States," *Educational Record,* Vol. 47, No. 1 (Winter, 1966), pp. 113-115.

"The Compact for Education, one of the most exciting innovations in this interesting period in American education, offers a valuable opportunity for strengthening the states and for developing a productive relationship among the three levels of government in solving the problems of education. It is important that the specific purpose of the compact be clearly understood . . . it would be foolish to assert that such a far reaching development is without its risks. . . ."

Anderson, Wayne M. *Cooperation Within American Higher Education.* Washington, D. C.: Association of American Colleges, 1964. 74 pp.

The author provides a listing of various types of cooperative arrangements including the institutions involved and persons to whom one may write for further information. Covers bi-lateral; city and area; state; regional; and national forms of cooperative projects. Includes selected references, appendices, and institutional and subject indexes.

Axelrod, Joseph and others. *Autonomy and Interdependence: Emerging Systems in Higher Education.* Washington, D. C.: American Council on Education, 1964. 89 pp.

This volume is comprised of five resource papers written as background for discussions at the Annual Meeting of the American Council on Education in 1964. The five topics deal in general with the conflicting concepts in higher education of "autonomy" and "interdependence." Topics covered include: "New Organizational Patterns in American Colleges and Universities"; "Consortia and Related Interinstitutional Arrangements in Higher Education"; "Interstate Cooperation and Coordination in Higher Education"; "National Organizations in Higher Education."

Benson, Charles S. *The Cheerful Prospect.* Boston: Houghton Mifflin, 1965. 134 pp.

A general discussion of the need for a change toward equalization and coordination of our nation's public school programs. Although the book is primarily concerned with public schools at the elementary and secondary levels, it has some pertinent arguments about government and higher education. The consensus is that both local and state reform are needed at the administration levels in order to eliminate the "geographical inequality of education," and "the uneconomical expenditure of funds."

Browne, Arthur D. "The Institution and the System: Autonomy and Coordination," *Long-Range Planning in Higher Education,* Owen A. Knorr, Ed. Boulder, Colorado: The Western Interstate Commission for Higher Education, 1964. pp. 39-51.

The case of autonomy versus coordination as applied to long-range planning is presented. The evidence points to a split decision, with each a winner if it is willing to pay a price. But the cost of winning is high, for it involves restraint and sacrifice which means the subjugation of personal interests to the welfare of the total educational enterprise.

Brumbaugh, A. J. *State-wide Planning and Coordination of Higher Education.* Atlanta, Georgia: Southern Regional Education Board, 1963. 45 pp.

This book represents a concise and short summary of the requirements for an effective state-wide planning and coordination agency. Several states are used as guidelines in describing the operation and functions of state planning boards. The author feels such an independent agency is needed in order to bring together the common objectives of both the citizens and the institutions of higher learning.

Cartter, Allan M. "The Shaping of the Compact for Education," *Educational Record,* Vol. 47, No. 1 (Winter, 1966), pp. 81-98.

The author traces the development of the Compact for Education from the introduction of the concept in Dr. Conant's *Shaping Educational Policy,* in 1964, through the early part of 1966. He concludes his remarks with a general assessment of the new organization.

Chambers, M. M. *Freedom and Repression in Higher Education.* Bloomington, Indiana: The Bloomcraft Press, Inc., 1965. 126 pp.

In the author's words he has "struggled to explain and present favorably the principle of individual freedom of choice and of institutional autonomy in higher education . . ." which to him are more important than centralized planning and administrative bureaucracy. Dr. Conant's book, *Shaping Educational Policy,* is heavily criticized on the grounds that Chambers feels diversity rather than unity ". . . is needed in a state's higher education policy, and at all costs our systems of higher education should steer away from any uniformity or regimentation of a bureaucratic nature."

——————. *Voluntary State-wide Coordination in Public Higher Education.* Ann Arbor, Mich.: The University of Michigan Press, 1961. 80 pp.

The author analyzes systems of non-compulsory planning and administering of state higher education in the hands of a formal agency. He asks some pointed questions as to the real benefit such organizations actually provide. He feels that "neither at the state level nor the national level do Americans want a rigidly structured 'European ministry of education' type of control of public colleges and universities." Special attention is given to the systems of higher education in California, Colorado, Indiana, Ohio, and Michigan.

Conant, James B. *Shaping Educational Policy.* New York: Mc-Graw-Hill, 1964. 135 pp.

Major concern is directed toward the recent trend of American higher education to turn to the federal government for advice and leadership. Conant feels that real bedrocks of higher education must be our state legislatures and trustees of private colleges and universities. Up to the present, however, few states have really effectively played a policy-determining role with the real objectives of the institution in mind. California and New York are cited as excellent examples of states which have adopted a system of a master plan in order to effectively plan and coordinate their systems of higher education.

Coons, Arthur G. and others. *A Master Plan for Higher Education in California, 1960-1975.* Sacramento, Calif.: California State Department of Education, 1960. 230 pp.

This volume, as prepared for the Liaison Committee of the Regents of the University of California and the California State Board of Education, forms a comprehensive analysis and projection of the state needs in higher education for a fifteen-year period. Includes index, tables, and appendices.

Coordinating Two-Year Colleges in State Education Systems. A Report of a Conference in Washington, D. C., May 16-17, 1957. U. S. Department of Health, Education, and Welfare, Office of Education. Washington: Government Printing Office, 1957.

The role of the state directors and supervisors of two-year colleges in coordinating these institutions in a state educational system is identified. Brief descriptions are included of the organization and scheme for operation and control of two-year institutions in sixteen states.

DeZonia, Robert H. "Coordination Among Higher Institutions in Wisconsin," *Educational Record,* Vol. 44, No. 3 (July, 1963), pp. 288-293.

The author presents a brief overview and analysis of the coordinating committee for higher education in Wisconsin. Although the committee has created certain frictions within the state, the author feels that it has contributed significantly to the advancement of higher education.

Donovan, George F., Ed. *College and University Interinstitutional Cooperation.* Washington, D. C.: The Catholic University of America Press, 1965. 158 pp.

Includes the papers and seminar reports from a workshop held at Catholic University in 1964. This volume broadly covers most areas of interinstitutional cooperation including the less publicized areas

of library cooperation, small college cooperation, religious cooperation, the role of the executive director, and cooperation among colleges for women. Selective bibliography and index.

Evan, William M. "The Organization-Set: Toward a Theory of
Interorganizational Relations," *Approaches to Organizational
Development,* James D. Thompson, Ed. Pittsburgh, Pa.: Uni-
versity of Pittsburgh Press, 1966. pp. 173-191.

Social science research on organizations has been concerned principally with intraorganizational phenomena. The relative neglect of
interorganizational relations is surprising in view of the fact that all
formal organizations are embedded in an environment of other organizations as well as in a complex of norms, values, and collectivities
of the society at large. The phenomena and problems of interorganizational relations are part of the general class of boundary-relations
problems confronting all types of social systems, including formal
organizations.

Glenny, Lyman A. *Autonomy of Public Colleges.* New York:
McGraw-Hill, 1959. 325 pp.

The author in this work presents a comprehensive description of the
existing patterns of coordination in higher education within states
until 1957. Through a process of extensive personal interviewing of
governors, college presidents, legislators, and state and university
administrative officers, the author is able to present a valuable picture of the various coordinating agencies and boards throughout the
United States. The book therefore attempts to enable legislators and
educators to have a better understanding of what type of coordinating
relationship within their state can best achieve a higher quality of
higher education while not sacrificing such concepts as autonomy and
freedom.

——————. "State Systems and Plans for Higher Education,"
Emerging Patterns in American Higher Education, Logan Wilson, Ed. Washington, D. C.: American Council on Education,
1965, pp. 86-103.

"Diversity continues to be cherished and encouraged by all, but today
the unlimited freedom of a college or university to pursue a self-
determined destiny is rapidly being curtailed among the public institutions and even has prospects of diminishing among the non-public
ones. At the state level the new watchwords are cooperation and
coordination, with institutional autonomy only within certain parameters. The classic condition of autonomy in higher education still
prevails in only ten states. . . ."

Green, Ralph T. "The Need for Coordination and Controls in the
Financing of State Institutions." *Proceedings of the 55th Annual
Conference of the National Tax Association, 1962.* Harrisburg,
Pa.: National Tax Association, 1963, pp. 476-82.

The author suggests that financial requests for institutions of higher
education be handled and controlled through a coordinating board

which then presents recommendations to the legislature. He contends that the legislative committees have not the time nor ability to handle the volumes of factual material that support requests, and are unable to truly differentiate between institutions.

Hanford, George H. "The Consortium Plan: New Hope for Weak Colleges," *Saturday Review,* Vol. XLVIII (January 16, 1965), pp. 52-3+.

A new concept in education for the small, academically weak colleges and for the scores of high school seniors who have been turned down by the college of their choice. The Consortium Plan suggests a co-operation association of colleges having three characteristics: (1) interchangeable freshman and sophomore offerings at all participating institutions; (2) specialized upper division programs on each campus which would comprehend the full range of the liberal arts; (3) automatic transfer of credits within the association.

Illinois Board of Higher Education. *A Master Plan for Higher Education in Illinois.* Springfield, Illinois: Board of Higher Education, July, 1964. 72 pp.

The plan is a comprehensive study of educational needs in public and non-public colleges and universities and other educational enterprises. It looks at questions such as: How should public colleges and universities be governed? What structure has to be provided for the most economical operation? To what extent is unified planning and coordination useful? To what extent should non-public institutions be involved in state-wide planning? Chapter 6 on financing and chapter 7 on organization and coordination are of special worth.

Jamrich, John X. "Interinstitutional Cooperation in Research and Instruction," *College and University,* Vol. 40, No. 1 (Fall, 1964), pp. 25-34.

The author lists five factors: educational adequacy and effectiveness; economic considerations; factor of human resources; recent general upsurge in emphasis on research; and the present rapid trend into interinstitutional cooperative efforts. He lists what he believes to be the valid reasons for cooperation and indicates possible implications and consequences of interinstitutional compacts.

——————— and Paul L. Dressel. "Surveys and Studies of Higher Education Needs and Problems," *Evaluation in Higher Education.* Boston: Houghton Mifflin Company, 1961, pp. 360-390.

A discussion of the growth, type, range, and sponsoring agencies of surveys and studies of higher education. The chief contribution of surveys is seen as justifying institutional budgets, adding confidence to decision-making, pointing up need for cooperation among institutions, and demonstrating need for expansion of higher education facilities. A comprehensive bibliography is included.

Leach, Richard H. and Redding S. Sugg, Jr. *The Administration of Interstate Compacts.* Baton Rouge, La.: Louisiana State University Press, 1959. 243 pp.

This work gives a detailed explanation of the Interstate Compact—its development, operation, and function. This rather new creature in public administration arose out of the concern for those areas of government which fall by default to the federal government if not occupied by the states. By remaining problem-oriented, and through effective cooperation on a regional level, these agencies have made significant contributions in such areas as education, natural resources, and specific public problems.

Litwak, Eugene and Lydia F. Hylton. "Interorganizational Analysis: A Hypothesis on Coordinating Agencies," *Administrative Science Quarterly,* Vol. 6 (March, 1962), pp. 395-426.

A theory of interorganizational coordination is presented based upon: (1) organizational interdependence, (2) level of organizational awareness, (3) standardization of organizational activities, and (4) number of organizations. The authors indicate a theory of limited conflict as opposed to traditional harmony theory.

Longenecker, Herbert E. "Some Implications of the Educational Compact Proposal for Higher Education," *Educational Record,* Vol. 47, No. 1 (Winter, 1966), pp. 106-112.

"Given the present situation, and the widespread apprehension and outright dissent almost unanimously expressed by those in higher education who have carefully and thoughtfully examined the implications of the proposed compact, one course of prompt action now seems relevant: states not yet aligned with the compact should be discouraged from joining it. . . ."

Martorana, S. V., James C. Messersmith, and Lawrence O. Nelson. *Cooperative Projects Among Colleges and Universities.* Office of Education, U. S. Department of Health, Education, and Welfare, Circular No. 649. Washington: Government Printing Office, 1961. 45 pp.

A broad coverage of various forms of institutional cooperation, this publication contains a descriptive analysis of the different types and cites examples. Areas covered are: Interinstitutional Cooperation; An Emerging Concept in Higher Education; Cooperation at Local, State, and Regional Levels; Planning for Cooperation in Higher Education; Helps and Hindrances to Cooperative Projects; and Principles and Guidelines for Establishing Interinstitutional Programs. Includes selected references, pp. 43-5.

Martorana, S. V. and Ernest V. Hollis. *State Boards Responsible for Higher Education.* Office of Education, U. S. Department of Health, Education, and Welfare, Circular No. 619. Washington: Government Printing Office, 1960. 254 pp.

Although dated, this volume is still an important study in the coordination of institutions of higher education. It is organized with a broad overview, analysis, and evaluation of state boards; a state-by-state analysis of the organization of public higher education in the United States; and a number of basic reference tables pertaining to state organization. Includes an appendix on the "Allocation of Operating Funds by Boards for Higher Education" authored by A. J. Brumbaugh and Myron R. Blee.

McConnell, T. R. "The Coordination of State Systems of Higher Education," *Emerging Patterns in American Higher Education,* Logan Wilson, Ed. Washington, D. C.: American Council on Education, 1965, pp. 129-141.

The author gives comprehensive coverage to the development and forms of the various state systems of coordination and cooperation in higher education. Areas covered include: Voluntary Systems; The Single Board; The Coordinating Board; Coordinated Planning; and Major Trends in Coordination. Includes select bibliography.

——————. *A General Pattern for American Public Higher Education.* New York: McGraw-Hill, 1962. 198 pp.

Discusses ways in which American colleges and universities can adapt to the "rising tide" of enrollment through state-wide coordination and cooperation. In suggesting such a plan, the diversity of the student and the various demands of our society must be accurately incorporated and represented. It is pointed out that coordination has a constructive role to play in providing both efficiently run schools and schools which optimize a state's given resources.

——————. *A Restudy of the Needs of California in Higher Education.* Sacramento, Calif.: California State Department of Education, 1955. 473 pp.

As prepared for the Liaison Committee of the Regents of the University of California and the California State Board of Education, this volume supplemented and replaced the original study of the needs of higher education in the state completed in 1948. Included in this extensive state study are: The Needs for Higher Education in California as Measured by the Population to be Served; The Functions and Programs of Higher Education in California; The Government, Administration, and Coordination of Public Higher Education; The Present Physical Plants and Future Plants Needed; and California's Ability to Support Higher Education.

McGrath, Earl J. and L. Richard Meeth, Eds. *Cooperative Long-Range Planning in Liberal Arts Colleges.* New York: Bureau of Publications, Teachers College, Columbia University, 1964. 108 pp.

This volume, published for the Institute of Higher Education, contains a broad coverage of cooperation in liberal arts colleges. Focusing on long-range planning, it includes articles by the editors, Paul L. Dressel, Algo D. Henderson, Walter E. Sindlinger, and others. Includes biographical sketches of the authors.

Medsker, Leland L. *The Junior College: Progress and Prospect.* New York: McGraw-Hill, 1960. 353 pp.

Is the junior college really a unique institution serving special functions which other institutions cannot serve effectively or do not serve at all? This is the basic question Dr. Medsker addresses himself in this study of some seventy-six two-year institutions in fifteen states.

Miller, James L., Jr. "The Two Dimensions of State-wide Higher Education Coordination," *Educational Record,* Vol. 43, No. 2 (April, 1962), pp. 163-167.

The author briefly describes different types of state coordination and coordinating bodies, but the primary concern is with the dimensions of coordination. The first is geographic coordination, termed horizontal due to its concern for providing equal educational opportunities across a state; the second is program coordination, termed vertical because it concerns itself with research and the pyramid of educational programs. Although effective coordination is not assured by a formal state organization, the author believes that more and more states are going to adopt some form of formal organization in the future.

Millet, J. D. "State Planning for Higher Education," *Educational Record,* Vol. 46, No. 3 (Summer, 1965), pp. 223-30.

The impression is conveyed that state planning for higher education is no bed of roses. It is not a field for the timorous, the anxious, the sensitive. But it is a field where much can be accomplished if all involved in public higher education will work together with intelligence, good will, and a sense of compromise. The alternative is a return to a jungle of political warfare in which reason is likely to play a small role and naked power will decide the issues.

Moos, Malcolm and Frances E. Rourke. *The Campus and the State.* Baltimore, Md.: The Johns Hopkins Press, 1959. 414 pp.

A study of the challenge and response in the day-to-day relationships between public institutions of higher education and American state governments. The authors believe that the trend toward administrative centralization within the states has been a major factor in introducing greater stress into relations between public colleges and universities and state government.

Reports on Higher Education. An Annotated Bibliography of Recent Reports of State Study Commissions and Other Official Agencies. Chicago, Ill.: The Council of State Governments, March, 1958. 15 pp. (Mimeographed)

An annotated bibliography of seventeen official state reports on higher education. The annotations include the major subjects covered in each report and a summary of the recommendations.

Strayer, George D. and Charles R. Kelleg. *The Needs of New Jersey in Higher Education 1962-1970.* A study prepared for the State Board of Education. Trenton, New Jersey: State Board of Education, April, 1962. 79 pp.

A plan is proposed for the structure of a system of higher education for the state. An estimate is made of the increased load to be carried by New Jersey public colleges and the state university for the years

1962-1970. A forecast is made of the investment in buildings, equipment, and other facilities New Jersey must make in order to provide for the predicted increase in enrollments to the fall of 1970.

The University of the State of New York, State Education Department. *The Regents' State-wide Plan for the Expansion and Development of Higher Education, 1964.* Albany, N. Y.: The University of the State of New York Press, April, 1965. 131 pp.

Every four years the State Board of Regents must submit a comprehensive plan for the orderly development of higher education. This is their first plan. The report is an extensive document covering every aspect of education and the peculiar organization and relationship of New York public and private schools. Report deals at length with the state needs to both the state and the society. Part IV deals with the institution plans and the means of the master plan to achieve identity, unity, and excellence throughout the university.

The University of the State of New York. *The State Education Department: Organization, Services, Functions.* Albany, N. Y.: The University of the State of New York Press, August, 1962.

A circular which describes the corporate power of the University of the State of New York and the Board of Regents. The functions and services of the State Education Department are listed. Contains a detailed organizational chart with a brief description of services available through each division of the State Education Department.

Wilson, Logan. *Diversity and Divisiveness in Higher Education.* Unpublished speech delivered to the American Association of Junior Colleges, March 1, 1966.

"Our system of higher education was organized largely in discrete units, with local boards, administrators, and faculties exercising considerable autonomy in the determination of their own means and ends. But the growing importance, expense, and interdependence of higher education institutions are forces exerting heavy pressures to change all this. . . ."

Wilson, Logan, Ed. *Emerging Patterns in American Higher Education.* A collection of essays. Washington, D. C.: American Council on Education, 1965. 292 pp.

This volume of essays is contributed by the nation's leading educators and scholars; it is a comprehensive overview of American higher education today. Directed primarily at organization and direction, it covers: the changing environment of higher education; institutional modifications; the emergence of state systems; voluntary arrangements; interinstitutional and interstate agreements; unified approaches to national problems; national associations in higher education; and national policy for higher education: problems and prospects. Primary emphasis is toward the emergence of a stronger national higher educational policy.

Advisory Panel, Joint State Government Commission. *Higher Education in Pennsylvania: Analysis of Problems with Proposals.* Pittsburgh, Pa.: The University of Pittsburgh, 1959.

Association of State-Supported Institutions of Higher Education in Colorado. *Progress Report to the General Assembly.* Denver, Colo.: The Association, 1962.

Coffelt, John J. *Self-Study of Higher Education in Oklahoma.* Oklahoma City, Okla.: Oklahoma State Regents for Higher Education, 1962-63. (a series of reports)

Committee on Higher Education. *Meeting the Increased Demand for Higher Education in New York State: A Report to the Governor and Board of Regents.* Albany, N. Y.: Board of Regents, November, 1960.

Dubbe, Alfred J. *Master Plan Study: Status Report—February 1, 1963.* Helena, Montana: University of Montana Systems of Higher Education, 1963.

Gibson, Raymond C. *Resources and Needs for Higher Education in Iowa, 1960-1970.* Des Moines, Iowa: Iowa 58th General Assembly, 1959.

Glenny, Lyman A. *The Nebraska Study of Higher Education.* Lincoln, Nebraska: Legislative Council Committee on Higher Education, 1961.

Hollis, Ernest V. *A Report of a Survey for North Dakota Research Committee and State Board of Higher Education.* Washington, D.C.: U. S. Office of Education, 1958.

Holy, Thomas C. *A Long-Range Plan for the City University of New York, 1961-1975.* New York: The Board of Higher Education, 1962.

Martorana, S. V. *Higher Education in South Dakota: A Report of a Survey.* Washington, D.C.: U. S. Office of Education, 1960.

Minnesota Liaison Committee on Higher Education. *Report for 1961-63.* Minneapolis, Minn.: The Liaison Committee, 1963.

Mississippi Legislative Education Study Committee. *Public Education in Mississippi: Report of Mississippi Legislative Study Committee.* The Committee, 1961.

Panel of Advisers. *Kansas Plans for the Next Generation.* Topeka, Kansas: Board of Regents, 1962.

Planning Committee. *Program for the General Differentiation and Coordination of Functions Among the State-supported Institutions of Higher Education in Colorado, 1963-1970.* Denver, Colorado: Association of State Institutions of Higher Education in Colorado, 1962.

Russell, John Dale. *The Final Report of the Survey of Higher Education in Michigan.* Michigan Legislative Study Committee on Higher Education, 1958.

Sorenson, Philip H., and Edward A. Podesta. *Long Range Planning for Higher Education in Idaho.* Menlo Park, Calif.: Stanford Research Institute, 1963.

Survey Staff. *Comprehensive Educational Survey of Kansas: Summary Report.* Topeka, Kansas: Kansas Legislative Council, 1960.

Texas Commission on Higher Education. *Public Higher Education in Texas 1961-1971.* Austin, Texas: The Commission, 1963.

The Governor's Commission on Education Beyond the High School. *The Report of the Governor's Commission on Education Beyond the High School.* Raleigh, North Carolina: The Commission, 1962.

Utah Coordinating Council of Higher Education. *Coordination of Utah Higher Education.* Salt Lake City, Utah: The Council, 1963.

Utah Coordinating Council of Higher Education. *The Coordination Study.* Salt Lake City, Utah: The Council, 1963.

Wisconsin Coordinating Committee for Higher Education. *A Plan to Extend the Outreach of Wisconsin's Public Colleges.* Madison, Wisconsin: The Coordinating Committee, 1963.

Section IV

The Federal Government and Higher Education: Old Answers Breed New Questions

Aly, B., Ed. *Government and Education.* Columbia, Mo.: Artcraft Press, 1961.

This work is a discussion debate manual prepared under the auspices of the Committee on Discussion and Debate Materials and Interstate Cooperation National University Extension Association. Broad scope and concentration on all levels of education. Bibliography pp. 425-438.

American Assembly. *The Federal Government and Higher Education.* Englewood Cliffs, N. J.: Prentice-Hall, 1960.

This study includes: (1) Purpose and policy in Higher Education; (2) Factual material on actual government practice and progress, pp. 74-5; (3) Issues in federal aid to higher education; (4) State and local government, pp. 158-163; (5) National goals quoted, pp. 176-7, 181-4.

American Council on Education. *Higher Education and the Federal Government: Programs and Problems.* 45th Annual Meeting, Chicago, 1962. Washington, D.C.: American Council on Education, 1963. 116 pp.

On the federal government and higher education up to the year 1962. Contains 10 chapters written by Nathan M. Pusey, David D. Henry, and McGeorge Bundy. Pusey's chapter presents the *Carnegie Study of the Federal Government in Higher Education.* Five separate chapters deal with the question of campus resource allocation. McGeorge Bundy concludes that "American higher learning is more not less free and strong because of federal funds."

————————. "Higher Education as a National Resource," *School & Society,* Vol. 91 (May 4, 1963), pp. 218-221.

The American Council on Education's proposal for a broad program of federal action to help expand and improve American education. The proposal is based on the premise that higher education constitutes a precious national resource essential to the achievement of national goals and the aspirations of individual citizens.

Arnold, Christian K. "Federal Support of Basic Research in Institutions of Higher Learning: A Critique," *Educational Record,* Vol. 45, No. 2, (Spring, 1964), pp. 199-203.

Primarily a discussion of the agency-to-individual grant/contract system of federal support for research, and an analysis of the report written under the auspices of the National Academy of Sciences entitled "Federal Support of Basic Research in Institutions of Higher Learning." The author suggests that although there are inherent dangers in this form of support for research, it is the best way at present, but the institutions must police themselves carefully. He also calls for alternatives to this policy.

—————. "Higher Education: Fourth Branch of Government?," *Saturday Review*, January 18, 1964, pp. 60-1+.

"The rather sudden growth of massive federal involvement in higher education since WWII has added an undigested new element to the relationship between universities and society. Our attempts so far to find solutions to these new problems have been engineering endeavors, not scientific ones. We have acted first and then tried to find rational justifications. Perhaps we ought to slow down long enough to take a look at where we are going before we find the path closed to alternate routes."

Babbidge, Homer D. and Robert M. Rosenzweig. *The Federal Interest in Higher Education*. New York: McGraw-Hill, 1962. 214 pp.

Describes the political and educational forces which formulate our government policy toward higher education. They state that political feasibility and expediency have been major determinants in such a policy and that federal programs are established not in the name of education but in the name of science, defense, etc. Book points up a chronic need for coordinating the policy and administration of government-higher education affairs.

Benson, Charles S. *The Economics of Public Education*. Boston: Houghton Mifflin, 1961. 580 pp.

This book is an analysis of the economics of education. The topic is dealt with as a sub-area of public finance and is basically an economics text. Under part two, "Sources of Public School Revenue," the total area of federal-state-local fiscal relations is discussed in detail. The text does not break the classification of education into sub-categories, but the problems of higher education are discussed.

Blum, Virgil C., Jr. *Freedom in Education*: Federal Aid for All Children. Garden City, N. Y.: Doubleday and Co., Inc., 1965. 235 pp.

Arguing that all children deserve freedom in education—the freedom to develop intellectually and expand their abilities—the author pursues the case for federal aid to parochial education. He contends that church-related institutions are a product of and asset to the diversity of the nation, and failure to equally support all institutions is leading toward a monolithic system.

Campbell, Roald F. and Gerald R. Sroufe. "Toward a Rationale for Federal-State-Local Relations in Education," *Phi Delta Kap-*

pan, Vol. XLVIII, No. 1 (September, 1965), pp. 2-7.

"We think that the increasing activity of the federal government in education demands examination and if possible the development of a rationale which would suggest the nature of an appropriate partnership among federal, state, and local governments as they relate to education. Our thesis follows: (1) the present situation is confused; (2) ours was a national federalism from the beginning; (3) there has been a gradual shift toward increased national federalism; (4) national federalism provides a basis for viewing recent policy developments in higher education; and (5) a rationale for policy sharing among national, state, and local governments is needed."

Carnegie Foundation for the Advancement of Teaching. *The Study of the Federal Government and Higher Education.* New York: The Carnegie Foundation, 1962.

The results of this self-study by 23 institutions, as compiled by the foundation, form one of the first serious studies into the effect of federal support on higher education. Areas covered include: the federal interest in higher education; security, health, and scientific research; people and institutions; issues and prospects. Includes appendices on the impact of federal tax policy on higher education and institutional self-study schedule as well as an annotated bibliography.

Chambers, Merritt M. *The Campus and the People.* Danville, Ill.: Interstate, 1960. 73 pp.

Centers on a theme that higher education is a public obligation. Solutions to possible coordination between institution and where the needed money will come from to finance our increasing systems are of special note. Chapters are composed of previously published articles in periodicals by eight authors.

——————. *Chance and Choice in Higher Education.* Danville, Ill.: The Interstate Printers and Publishers, 1962. 117 pp.

An arrangement of a dozen speeches and articles which first appeared during 1961-62 when the author was serving as executive director of the Michigan Council of State College Presidents, the voluntary agency of coordination among ten state universities and colleges in that state.

Chambers, M. M. *Freedom and Repression in Higher Education.* Bloomington, Indiana: The Bloomcraft Press, Inc., 1965. 126 pp.

In the author's words he has "struggled to explain and present favorably the principle of individual freedom of choice and of institutional autonomy in higher education . . ." which to him are more important than centralized planning and administrative bureaucracy. Dr. Conant's book, *Shaping Educational Policy,* is heavily criticized on the grounds that Chambers feels diversity rather than unity ". . . is needed in a state's higher education policy and at all costs our systems of higher education should steer away from any uniformity or regimentation of a bureaucratic nature."

DeBurlo, C. Russell, Jr. "Government and Education," *Review of Educational Research,* Vol. XXXV, No. 4 (October, 1965), pp. 361-9.

Survey of studies and works recently completed in this field. Areas surveyed include: Federal, State, and Local Governmental Responsibility for Education; Goals of the Federal Government and Higher Education; Composition of the Federal Interest and the Diversity of Higher Education; Legislative Process; Topical Breakdown and Analysis of Past and Present Government Support to Higher Education; The Effects of Federally Sponsored Research in Higher Education; and Future Relationship between Institutions of Higher Education and the Federal Government. Bibliography pp. 368-9.

Dobbins, Charles G., Ed. *Higher Education and the Federal Government*: Programs and Problems. Papers presented at the 45th Annual Meeting, Chicago, October, 1962. Washington, D. C.: The American Council on Education, 1963. 127 pp.

A broad coverage of the programs and problems involved in the relationship between higher education and the federal government. Includes remarks by both leaders of government and higher education which indicated at the time serious problems did exist but were the product of common concerns and could be solved. Select Bibliography, pp. 117-26.

Dubay, Thomas. *Philosophy of the State as Educator.* Milwaukee, Wisconsin: Bruce Publishing Co., 1959. 231 pp.

The book takes the position that a state must provide for and maintain its educational system. Mostly a broad, philosophical discussion using the term "state" to mean society or government in general. Deals with topics of natural law, state or educator, and the state's duties toward itself.

Engelbert, Arthur F. "Short-term Grants and Long-range Goals: The Dilemma of Federal Policies," *Educational Record,* Vol. 44, No. 2 (April, 1963), pp. 161-4.

The author describes some of the requisites necessary if governmental support of higher education is to be in the best interests of higher education. He contends that support must be more broadly based across the entire range of institutions and at more levels than just doctoral.

"Federal Tax Incentives for Higher Education," *Harvard Law Review,* Vol. 76 (1962), pp. 369-387.

As an alternative to federal aid and thereby inevitable control, the author suggests a tax credit to those who donate to higher education. It is pointed out that a tax credit is subtracted from the amount of tax due, while a deduction comes from gross income. A review of present tax provisions with novel suggestions for the "treatment of appreciated property," tax relief for persons bearing educational expense and "aid to student" are seen as attractive alternative measures to direct federal grants. Such a method would put aid in forms less in private control and more open to public scrutiny.

Fuller, Edgar. "Government Financing of Public and Private Education," *Phi Delta Kappan,* Vol. XLVII, No. 7 (March, 1966), pp. 365-372.

This article questions how much public education programs will be damaged if private and sectarian institutions continue to use and gain additional federal tax funds for their support.

Gardner, John W. *A.I.D. and the Universities*: Report to the Administrator of the Agency for International Development. Washington, D. C.: Agency for International Development, (April, 1964), 51 pp.

The author contends that there is a vital and impressive partnership between this, and like agencies of the government, and higher education. Includes a description of the "University's Role in Technical Assistance"; "The Aid-University Relationship"; "Participant Training"; "Research"; "University Contracts and Contract Administration"; "Personnel and Training"; and "Organization." Considering the present success and accomplishment of A.I.D., the author suggests that sometime in the near future, a semi-autonomous government institute be established to handle certain aspects of technical assistance—particularly relations with the universities. This, he contends, would enable greater long-term involvement in the combination of maximum operating efficiency with full accountability to government.

Goheen, Robert F. "Federal Financing and Princeton University," *Educational Record,* Vol. 44, No. 2 (April, 1963), pp. 168-180.

In describing the effects of federal support upon one institution, the author challenges the imbalance of support. However, he indicates that governmental programs must reflect public policy and that what is on trial is the American people's whole sense of organization, values, and purpose so that one of the principal jobs of educators is to bring the public to adequate awareness of the objectives, accomplishments, and requirements of higher education. Includes a list of Princeton's policies for sponsored research.

Green, Edith. *Education and the Public Good*: The Federal Role in Education. Cambridge, Mass.: Harvard University Press, 1964.

Draws attention to and points up the weaknesses of the diffusion of responsibility for educational programs in Congress. Urges consolidation of major acts within the federal government in order to ascertain the effects, achievements, and failures in our educational system.

"A Guide to Federal Aid for Higher Education," *College Management* (December, 1965), 23 pp.

This pamphlet is published by the editors of *College Management,* a new magazine for college administrators which started publication in early 1966. Its purpose is to enable educators as well as state officials to become acquainted with the tremendous volume of education-oriented legislation enacted by Congress during 1965. The volume gives a short description of the various educational achievements and, more important, where inquiries can be sent in order to obtain additional material.

Hanna, Paul R., Ed. *Education: An Instrument of National Goals.* Cubberly Conference, Stanford University, 1961. New York: McGraw-Hill, 1962.

Book consists of ten papers written for the general session of the 1961 Stanford University Cubberly Conference. In the opening chapter Paul Hanna asks whether education should be classified as consumption or investment. He traces the transition which has taken place and describes education as "an instrument of national purpose and policy." Three other chapters of special note are "New Goals for Science and Engineering"; "American Higher Education: Its Progress and Problems;" "The Role of Education in National Goals."

Harrington, Fred Harvey. "The Federal Government and the Future of Higher Education," *Educational Record*, Vol. 44, No. 2 (April, 1963), pp. 155-60.

Arguing that federal support is a necessary and good thing, the author indicates that institutions and individuals involved in higher education must now work separately and jointly to see to it that both needs, of higher education and of the public, are met. He contends that the question of government involvement and support is a moot one but that the terms of that involvement must continually be solved jointly.

Harris, Seymour E. *Challenge and Change in American Education.* Berkeley, Calif.: McCutchan Publishing Corporation, 1965. 346 pp.

Second in a series of three books edited by Seymour Harris based on the Seminars in American Education at Harvard University between 1958-1963. Three broad topics are presented: "Government and Education"; "Challenges in Educational Planning"; "Management of Colleges and Universities." The problems of multi-level governmental jurisdiction are presented by James E. Allen and Homer D. Babbidge, Jr. in a chapter on "State vs. Federal Power in Education." While the volume contains valuable commentaries by many educators, of special note are articles by: Robert Rosenzweig, Francis Keppel, Charles V. Kidd, and Andre Daniere.

————. *Education and Public Policy.* Berkeley, Calif.: McCutchan Publishing Corp., 1965. 347 pp.

The third in the trilogy on the American Education Seminars held at Harvard University deals in length with the issues involved in the increasing role federal aid is playing in educational policy. Authors Logan Wilson, Vernon Alden, and James McCormack agree that the need for federal aid to higher education is evident but that the criteria and objectives used for allocating this aid are the basic areas of disagreement. Philip H. Coombs and David Riesman address themselves to the area of planning in higher education. The last portion of the work is on the economic issues involved in the role of government to education.

—————————. *Higher Education: Resources and Finance.* New York: McGraw-Hill, 1962. 713 pp.

The economic issues facing higher education. The author defines and illustrates the nature of the problems and their various inter-relationships. He includes 170 points by way of summary and emphasis which provide the casual reader with a concise overview of the issues. Areas covered include: cost trends; pricing; scholarships; loans; government contributions; the management of productive funds; costs and economies; and faculty. Includes bibliographical notes and index.

—————————. *Higher Education in the United States: The Economic Problems.* Cambridge, Mass.: Harvard University Press, 1960. 247 pp.

This volume is the first of three books edited by Seymour Harris based upon Seminars on Higher Education held at Harvard University. It consists of papers written by different participants at the meetings and covers topics from "Pricing the Student Body" and "Government Aid" to "Economics and Educational Values." Of special note with regard to the government's role in higher education are the articles on "Federal and State Aid" by J. Paul Mather and "Higher Education and the Federal Budget" by Richard A. Musgrove. Musgrove saw early in the federal interest in education the need for aid in the form of direct assistance to the operating costs of institutions.

—————————. *More Resources for Education*: The John Dewey Society Annual Lecture, February 12, 1960. New York: Harper and Bros., 1960. 85 pp.

It is shown that expenditure in all levels of education have not kept pace with the use in other levels of expenditures by all levels of our government. Harris contends that higher education is by far a more complex problem in education than lower education and will require more than just additional money. Also that new mechanisms of finance as well as a redistribution of emphasis from local support to federal must come about in order to alleviate the tremendous burden placed on local and state governments.

Hester, J. M. "Private University in Our Tax Economy," *New York University Institute on Federal Taxation,* Vol. 21, No. 1 (1963).

James M. Hester, president of New York University, expresses genuine concern for the new position which our nation's private institutions have been placed in. He raises such questions as: Is there a place for private higher education in a society that has decided to provide higher education through taxation? Will increased taxation leave sufficient funds in private hands to enable us to finance private education? Do the private possessors of wealth and the corporations of this country understand and value free enterprise in higher education sufficiently to make the voluntary subsidies that would reduce the need for government subsidies and possible control? His suggestion is a more biennial tax structure for private donations and a realization by everyone that there is nothing antagonistic about public and private education, provided they can both survive.

Hill, W. W., Jr. "State Supported Student Loan Programs," *Proceedings, 55th Annual Conference of the National Tax Association, 1962*. Harrisburg, Pa.: National Tax Association, 1963, pp. 493-501.

Author indicates that, soon, 25 percent of all college students may be borrowing money for college expenses and up to 10 percent of all college expenses may be met by loans. A director of one of the nation's largest, private college loan companies, he urges local, state, and voluntary efforts in the area and argues against government involvement on a massive scale.

Hollis, Ernest V. "Federal Aid for Higher Education," *Proceedings, 55th Annual Conference of the National Tax Association, 1962*. Harrisburg, Pa.: National Tax Association, 1963. pp. 482-92.

Author analyzes the history and present situation of federal aid, concluding that the imperative need to keep higher education solvent and expanding justifies a further federal investment in the enterprise. This equalizes educational opportunity among the states without damaging essential authority or responsibility.

Hutchinson, Eric. "Politics and Higher Education," *Science,* Vol. 146, No. 3648 (November 27, 1964), pp. 1139-42.

"It can be argued that any national policy for education (even when flexibly applied) would represent an intrusion of the federal government into the affairs of many private institutions, which would see their autonomy being threatened. There is no doubt that this would be so, but the argument is weakened by the already critical dependence of many leading private universities on federal funds for science and engineering. Many universities appear to like the present hodgepodge arrangements, saying that they are the least intrusive method of support, but against this is the fact that this method makes any real policy impossible."

Jencks, Christopher. "Education: What Next?," *The New Republic,* Vol. 153, No. 16 (October 16, 1965), pp. 21-3.

"The problem of transforming poor schools is closely analogous to that which confronts the Office of Economic Opportunity in trying to promote 'community action' against poverty . . . . But when it was suggested that educational reformers would need similar powers, the Office of Education took the 'realistic' view that Congress and the National Education Association would never stand for it."

Kerr, Clark. "The Realities of the Federal Grant University," *Educational Record,* Vol. 44, No. 2 (April, 1963), pp. 165-7.

The author contends that the partnership between the federal government and higher education has been very productive, but now it is time to seek a wider and deeper relationship aimed at developing more institutions and improving areas other than just the sciences. Both education and government will need a better-coordinated voice.

Keezer, Dexter M. *Financing Higher Education 1960-1970.* New York: McGraw-Hill, 1959. 304 pp.

This volume, the McGraw-Hill 50th anniversary study of the economics of higher education in the United States, includes a broad coverage of the economic issues facing higher education by many noted scholars in the field. From a broad overview provided by Philip H. Coombs and Seymour E. Harris, the volume moves into specific issues, moving from the role of research to aspects of long-range planning to the role of private support. Of unusual interest is the chapter entitled "Outside the Conventional Structure," by Harold F. Clark.

Kidd, Charles V. *American Universities and Federal Research.* Cambridge, Mass.: The Belknap Press of Harvard University Press, 1959. 272 pp.

The author pursues the idea that large-scale federal financing of research has set in force irreversible trends that are affecting the nature of the universities, altering their capacities to teach, changing their financial status, modifying the character of part of the federal administrative structure, establishing new political relations, and changing the way research itself is organized. Believing these trends are good, the author develops these points from the research goals of the federal agencies and the functions of the universities to university participation in federal decisions. Includes bibliographical notes and index.

—————. "The Implications of Research Funds for Academic Freedom," *Law and Contemporary Problems,* Vol. 28, No. 3 (summer, 1963), pp. 613-624.

This article includes a discussion of "the effects on academic freedom of all outside funds for research . . . . The essential relationship of research support to academic freedom arises from the terms and conditions under which funds are provided and not from the source of funds. To be explicit, the earmarking of university funds or state appropriations for research to be conducted under tightly drawn terms and conditions can pose the same threats to academic freedom as can research funds provided by the federal government or by the large foundations."

Knight, Douglas. *The Federal Government and Higher Education.* Englewood Cliffs, New Jersey: Prentice-Hall, 1960.

This book is a compilation of papers that were required background reading for the participants in the Seventeenth American Assembly, May 1960. It is a thorough source of information about the growing activities of the federal government in colleges and universities.

Little, Kenneth J. "Higher Education and the Federal Government," *Higher Education,* Vol. XX, No. 2 (October, 1963), pp. 3-6.

Compares findings of 10 most recent major books. The author wonders if possibly the remarkable similarity in these books stems from the fact that fiscal policies of colleges and universities are a direct outgrowth of fiscal policies of the government rather than a genuine agreement with the role the government is presently playing in higher education. The author expresses concern that institutions are not keeping in mind that the basic responsibility of educational institututions is education and that programs of specialized service, research or other projects have their justification when they support the educational function.

―――――. "Higher Education and the National Purpose," *Educational Record.* Vol. 42, No. 3 (July, 1961), pp. 161-172.

This article, although outdated, is still of value in showing the interdependence between higher education and the national government. The author readily identifies the issues, i.e., maintain diversity of institutions and in sources of support safeguard institutions' independence and freedoms, improve coordination of government and educational policy.

―――――. *A Survey of Federal Programs in Higher Education—Summary.* Office of Education, United States Department of Health, Education, and Welfare, Bulletin 1963, No. 5. Washington: Government Printing Office, 1962. 56 pp.

Describes the federal programs, participating institutions, and the effects of the programs on the institutions. The survey, while comprehensive and thorough, is slightly dated. Bibliography, pp. 52-6.

―――――. "Trends Affecting Contemporary Educational Planning," *Journal of Higher Education,* Vol. 32 (April, 1961), pp. 192-198.

This article discusses the trends in higher education which center around two general problems: (1) problems of quantity—how to get teachers, classrooms, books, etc.: and (2) problems of quality—how to ensure that educational programs in the future will be of such strength as to stimulate the fullest possible development of human promise, and how to match the needs of a changing society.

McGrath, Earl J., Ed. *Universal Higher Education:* Institute of Higher Education. New York: McGraw-Hill, 1966. 247 pp.

Book is comprised of papers presented at the 1964 Institute of Higher Education of which five chapters are pertinent to government and higher education. These are: "Social, Political, Economic, and Personal Consequences" by Henry Steele Commager; "State Systems of Higher Education" by Thomas R. McConnell; "The Impact on Manpower Development and Employment of Youth" by Daniel Patrick Moynihan; "The Economic Aspects" by Algo D. Henderson; "English Higher Education: The Issues Involved" by A. D. C. Peterson;

and "Observations and Comments" by Frank H. Bowles. The volume contains a good anthology of material on major issues in higher education.

Medsker, Leland L. *The Junior College: Progress and Prospect.* New York: McGraw-Hill, 1960. 353 pp.

Is the junior college really a unique institution serving special functions which other institutions cannot serve effectively or do not serve at all? This is the basic question Dr. Medsker addresses himself in this study of some seventy-six two-year institutions in fifteen states.

Moore, Raymond E. "The Federal Government's Role in Higher Education," *Economics of Higher Education.* Office of Education, United States Department of Health, Education, and Welfare. Washington: Government Printing Office, 1962, pp. 202-218.

The history and extent of federal support to higher education. Assuming aid is needed we must decide whether states and institutions or students are to be the direct recipients. The problem of allocation among the various institutions and students is the other major issue to be resolved. In conclusion the author suggests that direct governmental expenditures and scholarships are superior to tax changes and loans. This article concisely presents an excellent picture of the issues which face government and education in the 60's.

—————. and D. W. Field. "Higher Education Facilities Act: A Status Report," *Phi Delta Kappan,* Vol. 46, No. 6 (February, 1965), pp. 277-9.

Moore and Field, both officials in the Bureau of Higher Education, have written a very informative and descriptive article on the Higher Education Facilities Act of 1963. By tracing our nation's past need for such a bill the authors point out its significance and effect on higher education. Statistical information along with illustrative comparisons between various states and institutions gives the article a very comprehensive outlook. The authors conclude that in enacting this legislation, Congress has shown a strong and abiding confidence in the ability of American higher institutions to frame reasonable financial programs.

Moos, Malcolm and Frances E. Rourke. *The Campus and the State.* Baltimore, Md.: The Johns Hopkins Press, 1959. 414 pp.

A study of the challenge and response in the day-to-day relationships between public institutions of higher education and American state governments. The authors believe that the trend toward administrative centralization within the states has been a major factor in introducing greater stress into relations between public colleges and universities and state government.

Munger, Frank J. *National Politics and Federal Aid to Education.* Syracuse, N. Y.: Syracuse University Press, 1962. 193 pp.

A factual presentation of the political factors, i.e., interest groups, legislative, government agencies in the problem of getting a program of federal aid to public education passed. Although the work is mostly on public education in general and lacks material since 1962, it does contain some very good descriptions of some political practices which don't meet the eye. Includes bibliography.

Muirhead, Peter P. "Federal Interest in Education," *College & University,* Vol. 39, No. 4 (Summer, 1964). 433 pp.

Muirhead of the U. S. Office of Education in this address discusses how federal resources can be utilized to enable universities to do a better job of educating. He establishes the theme that federal control is a myth and that we should begin to think of the federal government as belonging as much to our citizens as do their local and state government. He concludes that a utilization of our national resources must be achieved while protecting the local foundations and controls of our schools.

Mushkin, Selma J., Ed. *Economics of Higher Education.* Office of Education, United States Department of Health, Education, and Welfare. Washington: Government Printing Office, 1962. 406 pp.

A number of economists discuss the range of economic problems on which initial research has been accomplished and its implications to higher education; and suggest many areas where additional research is needed. Areas specifically covered include: College-Trained Personnel: Supply and Demand; Higher Education as an Investment in People; Financial Resources for Higher Education; and Economic Research in Higher Education. Introduction by Homer D. Babbidge, Jr., includes bibliographical notes with each article and various appendices.

———————— and Eugene P. McLoone. *Public Spending for Higher Education in 1970.* Chicago, Ill.: Council of State Governments, February, 1965. 68 pp.

As part of Project '70', a series of studies of state revenues and expenditures projected to 1970, this publication is concerned with questions raised if higher education needs are to be met in 1970. Contending that this is probably the fastest growing area of state expenditures during the coming five years, the authors look at present figures and, assuming certain economic and demographic conditions, project the necessities of 1970, and the amount of additional tax support required. Includes appendices showing statistics on a state-by-state breakdown.

National Academy of Sciences. *Basic Research and National Goals*: A Report to the Committee on Science and Astronautics, U. S. House of Representatives. Washington: Government Printing Office, March, 1965. 366 pp.

Composed of a series of articles by leading academicians and scholars, this volume sought to answer two broad questions presented by the House Committee on Science and Astronautics: (1) What level of federal support is needed to maintain for the United States a position of leadership through basic research in the advancement of science and technology and their economic, cultural, and military applications?; and (2) What judgment can be reached on the balance of support now being given by the federal government to various fields of scientific endeavor, and on adjustments that should be considered, either within existing levels of support or under conditions of increased or decreased over-all support?

Nevins, Allan. *The State University and Democracy*. Urbana, Illinois: University of Illinois Press, 1962. 171 pp.

An historical work on the four stages of development in our state and land-grant institutions, with special attention to their contributions to democracy. Current trends in enrollment, academic curriculum, and structure of public and private institutions. Of special note is chapter four on future trends.

Orlans, Harold. *The Effects of Federal Programs on Higher Education*. Washington, D. C.: The Brookings Institution, 1962. 353 pp.

By discussing specific grants and aid programs, the author arrives at three major conclusions: Federal programs have been increasingly concentrated in the sciences at large major universities while not diversifying impact. Such a trend has had beneficial results in the sciences at the sacrifice of the social sciences and humanities. The second area of concern is over the moot question "should funds be more widely dispersed?" In his last chapter, "Federal Control," the author suggests that institutions, in order to maintain autonomy and independence, should creatively determine their policy with regard to specific programs and presume these objectives at all costs.

—————————. "Federal Expenditures and the Quality of Education," *Science*, Vol. 142, No. 3600 (December 27, 1963), pp. 1625-29.

"What, since WWII, has been the relation of federal expenditures to the quality of higher educational institutions, of instruction, and of research, and what changes, if any, should be made in the present pattern of expenditures?" Mr. Orlans' conclusions are drawn mainly from a study of the effects of federal programs on departments of science, social science, and the humanities at thirty-six universities and colleges, undertaken by the Brookings Institution for the U.S. Office of Education.

Pierce, Truman M. *Federal, State, and Local Government in Education*. Washington, D. C.: Center for Applied Research in Education, 1964. 120 pp.

Viewpoint throughout the book is that education under the auspices of government has both reflected and strengthened concepts of individual freedom and opportunity. Issues such as control, goals, financing, and church and state are each discussed in regard to the role each branch of government will play in determining these issues. Bibliography, pp. 113-114.

Price, Don K. "Federal Money and University Research," *Science,* Vol. 151, No. 3708 (January 21, 1966), pp. 285-90.

". . . it would be naive to assume the present volume of government grants to universities for theoretical science could have been stimulated solely by a zeal for pure learning on the part of administrators or congressmen. The mixed motives that have led to this tremendous volume of appropriations are likely to lead to difficulties in the long run." The author goes on to discuss the problems likely to arise in the future and the dangers inherent in projections based on past experiences.

Reuther, Walter D. "The Challenge to Education in a Changing World," *Education and the Public Good.* Cambridge, Mass.: Harvard University Press, 1964.

A discourse on the challenge our nation's higher education must accept as a free nation. Stresses the interdependence of education and government in satisfying our chronic need for a unified effort in the area of education.

Rivlin, Alice M. *The Role of the Federal Government in Financing Higher Education.* Washington, D. C.: Brookings Institution, 1961. 179 pp.

Provides the reader with a background of the federal government's role in financing higher education by outlining the history of federal programs and pointing out the principal issues. Specific outlines are suggested on which a federal program might operate for aid to both student and institution.

Sliger, B. F. and Thomas R. Beard. "State Support of Public Higher Education," *Proceedings, 55th Annual Conference of the National Tax Association, 1962.* Harrisburg, Pa.: National Tax Association, 1963, pp. 464-76.

In answering the questions (1) how much should be spent on higher education, and (2) how much of the responsibility will fall upon state-supported—as opposed to private institutions of higher learning, the authors discuss state support in terms of: Higher Education and Optimum Resource Allocation; Needs and Means of State-Supported Higher Education; The Role of the States in Public Higher Education; and State Support vs. Higher Tuitions.

Sudermann, Frederick. *Federal Programs Affecting Higher Education*: An Administrative Reference Manual. Iowa City, Iowa: Inst. of Public Affairs, Division of Special Services, State University of Iowa, 1962. 775 pp.

This manual which is distributed by the American Council on Education is an exhaustive source of administrative and descriptive information on federal programs of all kinds. It serves the purpose of enabling institutions of higher education to become better acquainted with the opportunities available to them through government programs. The volume covers federal programs in the form of grants and loans for research equipment, facilities, fellowships, traineeships, and scholarships.

Sufrin, Sidney C. *Issues in Federal Aid to Education.* Syracuse, N. Y.: Syracuse University Press, 1962.

Although primarily oriented to elementary and secondary education, the author develops the idea that federal aid to education is indicative of a national interest in education. However, the assertion of a national interest demands more than federal funds; it must also include goals and standards and a new pattern of relationships between and among the various levels of government and private parties concerned with public education. Calls for expanded functions of the United States Office of Education. Includes index and bibliographical notes.

Trytten, M. H. "Higher Education as an Instrument of National Policy," *Current Issues in Higher Education,* G. Kerry Smith, Ed. The Proceedings of the Fourteenth Annual National Conference on Higher Education, Chicago, March, 1959. Washington, D. C.: Association for Higher Education, 1959.

The author contends that the educational process serves the nation best when it is true unto itself, but "only if there is a genuine awareness of national needs, and a willingness to meet those needs with initiative and imagination."

"Twenty-six Campuses and the Federal Government," *Educational Record,* Vol. 44, No. 2 (April, 1963), pp. 95-136.

This article provides a well-defined summary of data collected in a survey of the effect of federal funds on higher education, undertaken by the Carnegie Foundation for the Advancement of Teaching. Results did indicate that federal support of research exerted the greatest influence upon the participating institutions. Most institutions participating also felt that the force of the federal dollar was directed at immediate needs nationally and that programs should consider the long-range growth and improvement of higher education.

United States Congress, House Committee on Education and Labor. *The Federal Government and Education.* 88th Congress, 1st Session. House Document No. 159. Washington: Government Printing Office, 1963. 178 pp.

A study of all the educational programs which the government was involved in at that time. As submitted by Edith Green, chairman of the Special Subcommittee on Education, this document includes an analysis of the following: executive jurisdiction over educational programs; congressional jurisdiction over education legislation; facilities and equipment; support of students; support of teachers; curriculum strengthening; research in colleges and universities; federal institutions of higher education; federally impacted schools; miscellaneous programs; education of government personnel; programs in international education; and a summary of education expenditures. Study includes several supplements to text, a selected bibliography, and index.

————————, House Committee on Government Operations, Sub-committee on Research and Programs. *Conflicts between the Federal Research Programs and the Nation's Goals for Higher Education.* 89th Congress, 1st Session. Washington: Government Printing Office, 1965. 114 pp.

This publication provides a look at this pressing question. It is made up of the responses of the academic and other interested communities to an inquiry by Congress. Includes excerpts and replies from some of the 300 persons polled. Questions asked included the students, faculty, institutions, graduates, and the government.

Warner, J. C. "National Goals and the University," *Science,* Vol. 142, No. 3591 (October 25, 1963), pp. 462-64.

The author states that America faces a dilemma that calls for a careful re-thinking of national policy and university functions . . . . "The more fundamental problem, both for the universities and the nation, is the competition that has been engendered for the very highly trained and creative individuals who comprise the faculties of our universities."

Wayson, W. W. "The Political Revolution in Education, 1965," *Phi Delta Kappan,* Vol. XLVII, No. 7 (March, 1966), pp. 333-339.

The author says that educators should encourage and engage in more and more investigations of our educational policy processes. First, to understand and perhaps direct emerging changes in local, state, and federal roles; second, to develop systematic knowledge about the politics of education upon which to base a training program for future educational statement. The Compact for Education is cited.

Wesco, W. C. "Expansion and Excellence. A Choice in Higher Education?" *State Government,* Vol. 37 (1964), pp. 221-227.

In this article the author deals with two problems in higher education which have large implications for state finance and educational planning, as well as distribution of national research funds: (1) Enrollments will continue to mount rapidly, reaching into the post-graduate levels; (2) educational excellence must be maintained, expansion must not dilute quality.

Wilson, John T. "Higher Education and the Washington Scene, 1963," *Educational Record,* Vol. 44, No. 2 (April, 1963), pp. 145-54.

The author urges that the leadership of higher education involve themselves in the development of governmental programs in higher education in order to achieve some basic consensus on goals and direction which are in tune with the ideals and long-range needs of higher education. He cites the maze of political factors and items of national interest which complicate this process, and chides educators for failing to provide better guidelines for legislation and programs.

Wilson, Logan, Ed. *Emerging Patterns in American Higher Education.* A collection of essays. Washington, D. C.: American Council on Education, 1965. 292 pp.

This volume of essays is contributed by the nation's leading educators and scholars in American higher education today. Directed primarily at organization and direction, it covers: the changing environment of higher education; institutional modifications; the emergence of state systems; voluntary arrangements; interinstitutional and interstate agreements; unified approaches to national problems; national associations in higher education; and national policy for higher education: problems and prospects. Primary emphasis is toward the emergence of a stronger national higher educational policy.

—————. "A Better Partnership for the Federal Government and Higher Education," *Educational Record,* Vol. 44, No. 2 (April, 1963), pp. 137-144.

Contending that the growing interdependence between government and higher education calls for an unending assessment of the partnership, the author calls for a greater effort by institutions and organizations of higher education to address themselves to the nature and growth of this partnership. He cites the efforts being made by the American Council on Education.

—————. "A Better Partnership for the Federal Government and Higher Education," *Emerging Patterns in Higher Education,* Logan Wilson, Ed. Washington, D. C.: American Council on Education, 1965, pp. 272-281.

In this article Logan Wilson suggests certain major principles which he believes should be sought in developing the ideal "partnership" between the federal government and higher education. He sets forth six such principles, ranging from the broad encompassing one of allocating federal funds as to national interest and not regional pressure, to more concise principles such as the selectivity and merit qualifications of allocating federal programs.

Section V

The Effect of Federal Support on Allocation of Campus Resources

American Council on Education. *Higher Education and the Federal Government: Programs and Problems.* 45th Annual Meeting, Chicago, 1962. Washington, D. C.: American Council on Education, 1963. 116 pp.

The federal government and higher education up to the year 1962. Contains ten chapters written by Nathan M. Pusey, David D. Henry, and McGeorge Bundy. Pusey's chapter presents the *Carnegie Study of the Federal Government and Higher Education.* Five separate chapters deal with the question of campus resource allocation. McGeorge Bundy concludes that "American higher learning is more not less free and strong because of federal funds."

Arnold, Christian K. "Federal Support of Basic Research in Institutions of Higher Learning: A Critique," *Educational Record,* Vol. 45, No. 2 (Spring, 1964), pp. 199-203.

Primarily a discussion of the agency-to-individual grant/contract system of federal support for research, and an analysis of the report written under the auspices of the National Academy of Sciences entitled "Federal Support of Basic Research in Institutions of Higher Learning." The author suggests that although there are inherent dangers in this form of support for research, it is the best way at present, but the institutions must police themselves carefully. He also calls for alternatives to this policy.

——————. "Higher Education: Fourth Branch of Government?" *Saturday Review,* January 18, 1964, pp. 60-1+.

"The rather sudden growth of massive federal involvement in higher education since WWII has added an undigested new element to the relationship between universities and society. Our attempts so far to find solutions to these new problems have been engineering endeavors, not scientific ones. We have acted first and then tried to find rational justifications. Perhaps we ought to slow down long enough to take a look at where we are going before we find the path closed to alternate routes."

Baade, Hans W., Ed. *Academic Freedom: The Scholar's Place in Modern Society.* Dobbs Ferry, New York: Oceana Publishing, Inc., 1964. 217 pp.

Of the thirteen articles comprising this volume, three deal specifically with government involvement in some form and academic freedom.

"Academic Freedom and the Academic President" by Harold Dodels presents the view by a university president that this topic is relevant in all phases of university policy and "desirable, even indispensable." "Massive Subsidies and Academic Freedom" by Russell Kirk brings to light some revealing examples of how institutions have been compelled to sacrifice autonomy for less enduring but inviting alternatives. "The Implications of Research Funds for Academic Freedom" by Charles V. Kidd contends the partnership of institutions and government in meeting the increasing needs of higher education has been beneficial to both the academic community and to its freedom.

Babbidge, Homer D. and Robert M. Rosenzweig. *The Federal Interest in Higher Education.* New York: McGraw-Hill, 1962. 214 pp.

Describes the political and educational forces which formulate our government policy toward higher education. They state that political feasibility and expediency have been major determinants in such a policy and that federal programs are established not in the name of education but in the name of science, defense, etc. Book points up a chronic need for coordinating the policy and administration of government-higher education affairs.

Benson, Charles S. *The Cheerful Prospect.* Boston: Houghton Mifflin, 1965. 134 pp.

A general discussion of the need for a change toward equalization and coordination of our nation's public school programs. Although the book is primarily concerned with public schools at the elementary and secondary levels, it has some pertinent arguments about government and higher education. The consensus is that both local and state reform are needed at the administration levels in order to eliminate the "geographical inequality of education," and the "uneconomical expenditure of funds."

—————. *The Economics of Public Education.* Boston, Mass.: Houghton Mifflin, 1961. 580 pp.

Analysis of the economics of education. The topic is dealt with as a sub-area of public finance and is basically an economics text. Under part two, "Sources of Public School Revenue," the total area of federal-state-local fiscal relations is discussed in detail. The text does not break the classification of education into sub-categories, but the problems of higher education are discussed.

Cagle, Fred. *Federal Research Projects and the Southern University.* Atlanta, Ga.: Southern Regional Education Board, 1962. 97 pp.

Book is based on published information, extensive correspondence, and interviews with administrators of federal programs, university faculty members, and others. Cagle is quite concerned about the limited number of institutions which share in the bulk of federally supported research along with the lack of interrelationships between federal agencies and universities. Suggestions made which might alleviate this are: consideration of regional needs and established regional programs of research; "clearer policies and procedures for the interaction of government and universities"; and "the appointment of a liaison officer between the university and federal agencies."

Carnegie Foundation for the Advancement of Teaching. *The Study of the Federal Government and Higher Education.* New York: The Carnegie Foundation, 1962.

The results of this self-study by twenty-three institutions, as compiled by the foundation, form one of the first serious studies into the effect of federal support of higher education. Areas covered include: the federal interest in higher education; security, health, and scientific research; people and institutions; and issues and prospects. Includes appendices on the impact of federal tax policy on higher education and institutional self-study schedule as well as an annotated bibliography.

Daniere, Andre. *Higher Education in the American Economy.* New York: Random House, Inc., 1964. 203 pp.

Andre Daniere, a Harvard economist, has presented in this book the use of economic tools and principles in obtaining the goals of higher education. The theory of welfare economy, as it applies to higher education, is explained and discussed. The author feels the free market must remain "an operative device in the allocating of educational resources." He believes that a program of tuition loans to students would enable the institution to gain revenue while still leaving choices up to the student, and that such a program would provide public planning in higher education but yet private control of the institutions.

DeBurlo, C. Russell, Jr. "Government and Education," *Review of Educational Research,* Vol. XXXV, No. 4 (October, 1965), pp. 361-9.

Survey of studies and works recently completed in this field. Areas surveyed include: Federal, State, and Local Governmental Responsibility for Education; Goals of the Federal Government and Higher Education; Composition of the Federal Interest, and the Diversity of Higher Education; Legislative Process; Topical Breakdown and Analysis of Past and Present Government Support to Higher Education; The Effects of Federally Sponsored Research in Higher Education; and Future Relationship between Institutions of Higher Education and the Federal Government. Bibliography pp. 368-9.

DeVane, W. C. *Higher Education in Twentieth-Century America.* Boston, Mass.: Harvard University Press, 1965. 211 pp.

Chapter VI traces history of government involvement up to present and supplies reader with an articulated account of where government stands. Points out that control by agency is not the problem but rather whether or not institutions are profiting by present types of federal aid.

Dobbins, Charles G., Ed. *Higher Education and the Federal Government:* Programs and Problems. Papers presented at the 45th

Annual Meeting, Chicago, October, 1962. Washington, D. C.:
The American Council on Education, 1963. 127 pp.

A broad coverage of the programs and problems involved in the
relationship between higher education and the federal government.
Includes remarks by both leaders of government and higher education
which indicated at the time serious problems did exist but were the
product of common concerns and could be solved. Select bibliography, pp. 117-26.

Enarson, H. C. "Colleges with Sense of Direction Need not Fear
Federal Dollars," *College and University Business,* Vol. 38, No.
6 (June, 1965), pp. 46-9.

Article states that "federal pressures on colleges are intensive and
probably inevitable, but the institution that is sure of its own goals
has little to fear and much to gain from government involvement in
higher education." Shows four ways in which federal dollars are
opportunity dollars. Deals with questions of weakening institutional
control and the policing of grants and contracts when federal aid
is undertaken.

Engelbert, Arthur F. "Short-term Grants and Long-range Goals:
The Dilemma of Federal Policies," *Educational Record,* Vol.
44, No. 2 (April, 1963), pp. 161-4.

The author describes some of the requisites necessary if governmental
support of higher education is to be in the best interests of higher
education. Support must be more broadly based across the entire
range of institutions and at more levels than just doctoral.

"Federal Tax Incentives for Higher Education," *Harvard Law Review,* Vol. 76 (1962), pp. 369-387.

As an alternative to federal aid and thereby inevitable control, the
author suggests a tax credit to those who donate to higher education.
It is pointed out that a tax credit is subtracted from the amount of
tax due, while a deduction comes from gross income. A review of
present tax provisions with novel suggestions for the "treatment of
appreciated property," tax relief for persons bearing educational expense, and "aid to student" are seen as attractive alternative measures
to direct federal grants. He believes that such a method would put
aid in forms less in private control and more open to public scrutiny.

Fuller, Edgar. "Government Financing of Public and Private Education," *Phi Delta Kappan,* Vol. XLVII, No. 7 (March, 1966).
pp. 365-372.

This article questions how much public education programs will be
damaged if private and sectarian institutions continue to use and
gain additional federal tax funds for their support.

Gardner, John W. *A.I.D. and the Universities:* Report to the Administrator of the Agency for International Development. Washington, D. C.: Agency for International Development, April,
1964. 51 pp.

The author contends that there is a vital and impressive partnership between this and like agencies of the government, and higher education. Includes a description of the "University's Role in Technical Assistance"; "The A.I.D.-University Relationship"; "Participant Training"; "Research"; "University Contracts and Contract Administration"; "Personnel and Training"; and "Organization." Considering the present success and accomplishment of A.I.D., the author suggests that sometime in the near future, a semi-autonomous government institute be established to handle certain aspects of technical assistance—particularly relations with the universities. This, he contends, would enable greater long-term involvement in the combination of maximum operating efficiency with full accountability to government.

Goheen, Robert F. "Federal Financing and Princeton University," *Educational Record,* Vol. 44, No. 2 (April, 1963), pp. 168-80.
In describing the effects of federal support upon one institution, the author challenges the imbalance of support. However, he indicates that governmental programs must reflect public policy and that what is on trial is the American people's whole sense of organization, values, and purpose so that one of the principal jobs of educators is to bring the public to adequate awareness of the objectives, accomplishments, and requirements of higher education. Includes a list of Princeton's policies for sponsored research.

"A Guide to Federal Aid for Higher Education," *College Management* (December, 1965). 23 pp.
This pamphlet is published by the editors of *College Management,* a new magazine for college administrators which started publication in early 1966. Its purpose is to enable educators as well as state officials to become acquainted with the tremendous volume of education-oriented legislation enacted by Congress during 1965. The volume gives a short description of the various educational achievements and, more important, where inquiries can be sent in order to obtain additional material.

Harrington, Fred Harvey. "The Federal Government and the Future of Higher Education," *Educational Record,* Vol. 44, No. 2 (April, 1963), pp. 155-60.
Arguing that federal support is a necessary and good thing, the author indicates that institutions and individuals involved in higher education must now work separately and jointly to see to it that both needs of higher education and the public are met. He contends that the question of government involvement and support is a moot one but that the terms of that involvement must continually be solved jointly.

Harris, Seymour E. *Challenge and Change in American Education.* Berkeley, Calif. McCutchan Publishing Corporation, 1965. 346 pp.
Second in a series of three books edited by Seymour Harris based

171

on the Seminars in American Education at Harvard University between 1958-1963. Three broad topics are presented: "Government and Education"; "Challenges in Educational Planning"; "Management of Colleges and Universities." The problems of multi-level governmental jurisdiction are presented by James E. Allen and Homer D. Babbidge, Jr. in a chapter on "State vs. Federal Power in Education." While the volume contains commentaries by many educators, of special note are articles by: Robert Rosenzweig, Francis Keppel, Charles V. Kidd, and Andre Daniere.

——————. *Education and Public Policy.* Berkeley, Calif.: McCutchan Publishing Corp., 1965. 347 pp.

The third in the trilogy on the American Education Seminars held at Harvard University deals in length with the issues involved in the increasing role federal aid is playing in educational policy. Authors Logan Wilson, Vernon Alden, and James McCormack agree that the need for federal aid to higher education is evident but that the criteria and objectives used for allocating this aid are the basic areas of disagreement. Philip H. Coombs and David Riesman address themselves to the area of planning in higher education. The last portion of the work is on the economic issues involved in the role of government to education.

——————. *Higher Education: Resources and Finance.* New York: McGraw-Hill, 1962. 713 pp.

The economic issues facing higher education. The author defines and illustrates the nature of the problems and their various interrelationships. He includes 170 points by way of summary and emphasis which provide the casual reader with a concise overview of the issues. Areas covered include: cost trends; pricing; scholarships; loans; government contributions; the management of productive funds; costs and economies; and faculty. Includes bibliographical notes and index.

——————. *Higher Education in the United States: The Economic Problems.* Cambridge, Mass.: Harvard University Press, 1960. 247 pp.

This volume is the first of three books edited by Seymour Harris based upon Seminars on Higher Education held at Harvard University. It consists of papers written by different participants at the meetings and covers topics from "Pricing the Student Body" and "Government Aid" to "Economics and Educational Values." Of special note, with regard to government role in higher education, articles on "Federal and State Aid" by J. Paul Mather, and "Higher Education and the Federal Budget" by Richard A. Musgrove. Musgrove saw early in the federal interest in education the need for aid in the form of direct assistance to the operating costs of institutions.

Hollis, Ernest V. "Federal Aid for Higher Education," *Proceedings, 55th Annual Conference of the National Tax Association, 1962.* Harrisburg, Pa.: National Tax Association, 1963, pp. 482-92.

Author analyzes the history and present situation of federal aid, concluding that the imperative need to keep higher education solvent and expanding justifies a further federal investment in the enterprise. This equalizes educational opportunity among the states without damaging essential authority or responsibility.

Jencks, Christopher. "Education: What Next?" *The New Republic,* Vol. 153, No. 16 (October 16, 1965), pp. 21-3.

"The problem of transforming small schools is closely analogous to that which confronts the Office of Economic Opportunity in trying to promote 'community action' against poverty . . . . But when it was suggested that educational reformers would need similar powers, the Office of Education took the 'realistic' view that Congress and the National Education Association would never stand for it."

Keezer, Dexter M. *Financing Higher Education 1960-1970.* New York: McGraw-Hill, 1959. 304 pp.

This volume, the McGraw-Hill 50th anniversary study of the economics of higher education in the United States, includes a broad coverage of the economic issues facing higher education by many of the most noted scholars in the field. From a broad overview provided by Philip H. Coombs and Seymour E. Harris, the volume moves into specific issues, moving from the role of research to aspects of long-range planning to the role of private support. Of unusual interest is the chapter entitled "Outside the Conventional Structure," by Harold F. Clark.

Kerr, Clark. "The Realities of the Federal Grant University," *Educational Record,* Vol. 44, No. 2 (April, 1963), pp. 165-7.

The author contends that the partnership between the federal government and higher education has been very productive, but now it is time to seek a wider and deeper relationship aimed at developing more institutions and improving areas other than just the sciences. Both education and government will need a better-coordinated voice.

—————. *The Uses of the University:* Godkin Lectures. Cambridge, Mass.: Harvard University Press, 1963. 140 pp.

This noted contribution to higher education, written by the president of the conglomerate University of California, contains material on the actual effect of massive subsidies and a university's subsequent position when federal aid is given to it in any form. Of special interest is chapter two entitled "Federal Grant Universities."

Kidd, Charles V. *American Universities and Federal Research.* Cambridge, Mass.: The Belknap Press of Harvard University Press, 1959. 272 pp.

The author pursues the idea that large-scale federal financing of research has set in force irreversible trends that are affecting the nature of the universities, altering their capacities to teach, changing their financial status, modifying the character of part of the federal administrative structure, establishing new political relations, and changing the way research itself is organized. Believing these trends are good, the author develops these points from the research goals of the federal agencies and the functions of the universities to university participation in federal decisions. Includes bibliographical notes and index.

——————. "The Implications of Research Funds for Academic Freedom," *Law and Contemporary Problems,* Vol. 28, No. 3 (Summer, 1963), pp. 613-624.

This article includes a discussion of "the effects on academic freedom of all outside funds for research . . . . The essential relationship of research support to academic freedom arises from the terms and conditions under which funds are provided and not from the source of the funds. To be explicit, the earmarking of university funds or state appropriations for research to be conducted under tightly drawn terms and conditions can pose the same threats to academic freedom as can research funds provided by the federal government or by the large foundations."

Kirk, R. "Massive Subsidies and Academic Freedom," *Law and Contemporary Problems,* Vol. 28, No. 3 (Summer, 1963), pp. 607-12.

Professor Kirk is more than critical of the infringement and eroding away of academic freedom which has taken place because of federal subsidies and grants to institutions of higher learning. He uses several anonymous case studies of universities to point out that "the preferences and value judgments of the administration of foundations and governmental agencies" are being carried out by indirect force. Douglas Knight, president of Duke University, and himself agree that centralization of existing government agencies is not the answer to the evident incoherence in federal aid. In general, he questions if a sacrifice in freedom is not too high a price to pay for governmental and foundational subsidies.

Knight, Douglas. *The Federal Government and Higher Education.* Englewood Cliffs, New Jersey: Prentice-Hall, 1960.

This book is a compilation of papers that were required background reading for the participants in the Seventeenth American Assembly, May 1960. It is a thorough source of information about the growing activities of the federal government in colleges and universities.

Little, Kenneth J. "Higher Education and the Federal Government," *Higher Education,* Vol. XX, No. 2 (October, 1963), pp. 3-6.

Compares findings of ten recent books. The author wonders if possibly the remarkable similarity in these books stems from the fact that fiscal policies of colleges and universities are a direct outgrowth of fiscal policies of the government rather than a genuine agreement with the role the government is presently playing in higher education. The author expresses concern that institutions are not keeping in mind that the basic responsibility of educational institutions is education and that programs of specialized service, research, or other projects have their justification when they support the educational function.

——————. *A Survey of Federal Programs in Higher Education—Summary.* Office of Education, United States Department of Health, Education, and Welfare, Bulletin 1963, No. 5. Washington: Government Printing Office, 1962. 56 pp.

Describes the federal programs, participating institutions, and the effects of the programs on the institutions. The survey, while comprehensive and thorough, is slightly dated. Bibliography, pp. 52-6.

Maramaduke, Arthur S. "Can We Live with Federal Funds?" *College Board Review,* No. 59 (Spring, 1966), pp. 7-10.

This article deals with the threat of governmental control of this nation's colleges, especially in conjunction with the 600-700 million dollars in federal and state funds to become available to college students in the next three years.

Monill, James L. *The Ongoing State University.* Minneapolis, Minn.: University of Minnesota Press, 1960. 137 pp.

As past president of one of our nation's largest universities, the University of Minnesota, the author traces the development of the land-grant institution to its present position as a "catalyst" of state initiative and investment in educational opportunity and research. Chapters on "Higher Education and Federal Government" and "The Responsibility of the State to its University" deal with a large university's problems and alternatives in meeting a period of unusual challenge in our nation's history.

Moore, Raymond E. "The Federal Government's Role in Higher Education," *Economics of Higher Education.* Office of Education, United States Department of Health, Education, and Welfare. Washington: Government Printing Office, 1962. pp. 202-218.

The author in a brief but complete manner covers the history and extent of federal support to higher education. Assuming aid is needed, we must decide whether states and institutions or students are to be the direct recipients. The problem of allocation among the various institutions and students is the other major issue to be resolved. In conclusion the author suggests that direct governmental expenditures and scholarships are superior to tax changes and loans. This article concisely presents an excellent picture of the issues which face government and education in the sixties.

—————— and D. W. Field. "Higher Education Facilities Act: A Status Report," *Phi Delta Kappan,* Vol. 46, No. 6 (February, 1965), pp. 277-9.

Moore and Field, both officials in the Bureau of Higher Education, have written a very informative and descriptive article on the Higher Education Facilities Act of 1963. By tracing our nation's past need for such a bill the authors point out its significance and effect on higher education. Statistical information and illustrative comparisons between various states and institutions give the article a very comprehensive outlook. The authors conclude that in enacting this legislation, Congress has shown a strong and abiding confidence in the ability of American higher education institutions to frame reasonable financial programs.

Muirhead, Peter P. "Federal Interest in Education," *College & University,* Vol. 39, No. 4 (Summer, 1964), 433 pp.

Muirhead of the U. S. Office of Education in this address discusses how federal resources can be utilized to enable universities to do a better job of educating. He establishes the theme that federal control is a myth and that we should begin to think of the federal government as belonging as much to our citizens as do their local and state government. He concludes that a utilization of our national resources must be achieved while protecting the local foundations and controls of our schools.

Munster, Joseph H., Jr. and Justin C. Smith. "The University in the Market Place," *Journal of Higher Education,* Vol. XXXV, No. 8 (November, 1964), pp. 417-425.

A warning to all institutions seeking to work with the federal government to realize that they are actually dealing with the federal government, and that each agency is likely to have its own policy with respect to costs, patents, security, and so on. Also, the institutions should know their own policies with respect to recurring problems in order that individual department heads may take the initiative in negotiating certain concessions from the various supporting agencies.

Mushkin, Selma J., Ed. *Economics of Higher Education.* Office of Education, United States Department of Health, Education, and Welfare. Washington: Government Printing Office, 1962. 406 pp.

A number of eminent economists discuss the range of economic problems on which initial research has been accomplished and its implications to higher education, and suggest many areas where additional research is needed. Areas specifically covered include: College-Trained Personnel: Supply and Demand; Higher Education as an Investment in People; Financial Resources for Higher Education; and Economic Research in Higher Education. Introduction by Homer D. Babbidge, Jr. Includes bibliographical notes with each article and various appendices.

————— and Eugene P. McLoone. *Public Spending for Higher Education in 1970.* Chicago, Ill.: Council of State Governments, February, 1965. 68 pp.

As part of Project '70', a series of studies of state revenues and expenditures projected to 1970, this publication is concerned with questions raised if higher education needs are to be met in 1970. Contending that this is probably the fastest growing area of state expenditures during the coming five years, the authors look at present figures and, assuming certain economic and demographic conditions, project the necessities of 1970, and the amount of additional tax support required. Includes appendices showing statistics on a state-by-state breakdown.

National Academy of Sciences. *Basic Research and National Goals*: A Report to the Committee on Science and Astronautics, U. S. House of Representatives. Washington: Government Printing Office, March, 1965. 366 pp.

Composed of a series of articles by leading academicians and scholars, this volume sought to answer two broad questions presented by the House Committee on Science and Astronautics: (1) What level of federal support is needed to maintain for the United States a position of leadership through basic research in the advancement of science and technology and their economic, cultural, and military applications? and (2) What judgment can be reached on the balance of support now being given by the federal government to various fields of scientific endeavor, and on adjustments that should be considered, either within existing levels of support or under conditions of increased or decreased over-all support?

Orlans, Harold. *The Effects of Federal Programs on Higher Education*. Washington, D. C.: The Brookings Institution, 1962. 353 pp.

By discussing specific grants and aid programs the author arrives at three major conclusions: Federal programs have been increasingly concentrated in the sciences at large major universities while not diversifying its impact. Such a trend has had beneficial results in the sciences at the sacrifice of the social sciences and humanities. The second area of concern is over the moot question of "should funds be more widely dispersed?" In his last chapter, "Federal Control," the author suggests that institutions in order to maintain autonomy and independence should creatively determine their policy with regard to specific programs and presume these objectives at all costs.

——————. "Federal Expenditures and the Quality of Education," *Science,* Vol. 142, No. 3600 (December 27, 1963), pp. 1625-29.

"What, since WWII, has been the relation of federal expenditures to the quality of higher educational institutions, of instruction, and of research, and what changes, if any, should be made in the present pattern of expenditures? Mr. Orlans' conclusions are drawn mainly from a study of the effects of federal programs on departments of science, social science, and the humanities at 36 universities and colleges, undertaken by the Brookings Institution for the U. S. Office of Education.

Price, Don K. "Federal Money and University Research," *Science,* Vol. 151, No. 3708 (January 21, 1966), pp. 285-90.

"It would be naive to assume the present volume of government grants to universities for theoretical science could have been stimulated solely by a zeal for pure learning on the part of administrators or congressmen. The mixed motives that have led to this tremendous volume of appropriations are likely to lead to difficulties in the long run." The author goes on to discuss the problems likely to arise in the future and the dangers inherent in projections based on past experiences.

Rivlin, Alice M. *The Role of the Federal Government in Financing Higher Education.* Washington, D. C.: Brookings Institution, 1961. 179 pp.

Provides the reader with a background of the federal government's role in financing higher education by outlining the history of federal programs and pointing out the principal issues. Specific outlines are suggested on which a federal program might operate for aid to both student and institution.

Sudermann, Frederick. *Federal Programs Affecting Higher Education*: An Administrative Reference Manual. Iowa City, Iowa: Inst. of Public Affairs, Division of Special Services, State University of Iowa, 1962. 775 pp.

This manual which is distributed by the American Council on Education is an exhaustive source of administrative and descriptive information on federal programs of all kinds. It serves the purpose of enabling institutions of higher education to become better acquainted with the opportunities available to them through government programs. The volume covers federal programs in the form of grants and loans for research, equipment, facilities, fellowships, traineeships, and scholarships.

Sufrin, Sidney C. *Administering the National Defense Education Act.* Syracuse, New York: Syracuse University Press, 1963. 76 pp.

In this book Professor Sufrin has attempted to alleviate and effectively avert many of the problems of coordinating local, state, and federal levels of government in accomplishing the purposes of the NDEA. In doing this the author has written a very scholarly text which identifies the issues involved in the NDEA and the total of federal aid for higher education. He discusses such topics as "Power —Laws and Extent" and the idea of "categorical and general aid." While a great deal of the emphasis is on secondary and elementary education, the topic of higher education is interwoven in the analysis.

"Twenty-six Campuses and the Federal Government," *Educational Record,* Vol. 44, No. 2 (April, 1963), pp. 95-136.

This article provides a well-defined summary of data collected in a survey of the effect of federal funds on higher education, undertaken by the Carnegie Foundation for the Advancement of Teaching. Results did indicate that federal support of research exerted the greatest influence upon the participating institutions. Most institutions participating also felt that the force of the federal dollar was directed at immediate needs nationally and that programs should consider the long-range growth and improvement of higher education.

United States Congress, House Committee on Education and Labor. *The Federal Government and Education.* 88th Congress, 1st Session. House Document No. 159. Washington: Government Printing Office, 1963. 178 pp.

A study of all the educational programs which the government was involved in at that time. As submitted by Edith Green, chairman of the Special Subcommittee on Education, this document includes an analysis of the following: executive jurisdiction over educational programs; congressional jurisdiction over education legislation; facilities and equipment; support of students; support of teachers; curriculum strengthening; research in colleges and universities; federal institutions of higher education; federally impacted programs in international education; and a summary of education expenditures. Study includes several supplements to text, a selected bibliography, and index.

————————, House Committee on Government Operations, Subcommittee on Research and Programs. *Conflicts between the Federal Research Programs and the Nation's Goals for Higher Education.* 89th Congress, 1st Session. Washington: Government Printing Office, 1965. 114 pp.

This publication provides a valuable look at this pressing question. It is made up of the responses of the academic and other interested communities to an inquiry by Congress. Includes excerpts and replies from some of the 300 persons polled. Questions asked included the students, faculty, institutions, graduates, and the government.

Wesco, W. C. "Expansion and Excellence. A Choice in Higher Education?," *State Government,* Vol. 37 (1964), pp. 221-227.

In this article the author deals with two problems in higher education which have large implications for state finance and educational planning, as well as distribution of national research funds: (1) Enrollments will continue to mount rapidly, reaching into the postgraduate levels; (2) educational excellence must be maintained; expansion must not dilute quality.

Wilson, Logan, Ed. *Emerging Patterns in American Higher Education.* A collection of essays. Washington, D. C.: American Council on Education, 1965. 292 pp.

This volume of essays is contributed by the nation's leading educators and scholars; it is a comprehensive overview of American higher education today. Directed primarily at organization and direction, it covers: the changing environment of higher education; institutional modifications; the emergence of state systems; voluntary arrangements; interinstitutional and interstate agreements; unified approaches to national problems; national associations in higher education; and national policy for higher education: problems and prospects. Primary emphasis is toward the emergence of a stronger national higher educational policy.

—————————. "A Better Partnership for the Federal Government and Higher Education," *Educational Record,* Vol. 44, No. 2 (April, 1963), pp. 137-144.

Contending that the growing interdependence between government and higher education calls for an unending assessment of the partnership, the author calls for a greater effort by institutions and organizations of higher education to address themselves to the nature and growth of this partnership. He cites the efforts being made by the American Council on Education.

Section VI

The Compact for Education

Allen, James. "The Compact: New Strength for the States," *Educational Record,* Vol. 47, No. 1 (Winter, 1966), pp. 113-115.
"The Compact for Education, one of the most exciting innovations in this interesting period in American education, offers a valuable opportunity for strengthening the states and for developing a productive relationship among the three levels of government in solving the problems of education. It is important that the specific purpose of the compact be clearly understood . . . it would be foolish to assert that such a far-reaching development is without its risks. . . ."

Berg, Rodney, "The Compact and the Junior College," *Junior College Journal,* Vol. 36, No. 8 (May, 1966), pp. 8-9.
As president of a junior college and member of the steering committee of the compact, Mr. Berg sees as significant the fact that a study of junior college development and expansion has high priority in the compact. The compact, with its proposed network of information exchange, is seen as playing a potentially powerful role in solving some of the emerging junior college problems.

Cartter, Allan M. "The Shaping of the Compact for Education," *Educational Record,* Vol. 47, No. 1 (Winter, 1966), pp. 81-98.
The author traces the development of the Compact for Education from the introduction of the concept in Dr. Conant's *Shaping Educational Policy,* in 1964, through the early part of 1966. He concludes his remarks with a general assessment of the new organization.

Chafee, John H. "The Compact on Education is a Reality," *Junior College Journal,* Vol. 36, No. 8 (May, 1966), pp. 6-9.
Chaffee, as chairman of the new Compact for Education, summarizes the highlights of the causes which brought the compact into being, and some of the results he hopes it will achieve. He emphasizes that the compact will be a happy medium between the independent educational views of the states, and the influence of the federal government. By playing a coordinating role rather than policy-making, it will help the states coordinate their educational efforts, and help the federal government be more sensitive to the educational needs of the states.

Chambers, M. M. *Freedom and Repression in Higher Education.* Bloomington, Indiana: The Bloomcraft Press, Inc., 1965. 126 pp.

In the author's words, he has "struggled to explain and present favorably the principle of individual freedom of choice and of institutional autonomy in higher education . . ." which to him are more important than centralized planning and administrative bureaucracy. Dr. Conant's book, *Shaping Educational Policy,* is heavily criticized on the grounds that Chambers feels diversity rather than unity ". . . is needed in a state's higher education policy, and at all costs our systems of higher education should steer away from any uniformity or regimentation of a bureaucratic nature."

Cohodes, Aaron. "Compact for Education Slated for December Start: Sanford," *Nation's Schools,* Vol. 76, No. 5 (November, 1965), pp. 55-56.

A summary of the Kansas City conference on the proposed Compact for Education. It deals primarily with the views expressed by some of the 19 governors, 50 state legislators, and 250 educators who attended.

"Compact for Education," *Educational Record,* Vol. 47, No. 1 (Winter, 1966), pp. 116-121.

A reprint of the preamble and articles of the Compact for Education.

Conant, James B. "How the Compact can Assist Universities," *Educational Record,* Vol. 47, No. 1 (Winter, 1966), pp. 99-105.

"The newly created organization can help the private and public colleges and universities of the nation. . . . One thing seems certain— what happens will depend on the attitude of the leaders of education at all levels."

——————. *Shaping Educational Policy.* New York: McGraw-Hill, 1964. 135 pp.

Major concern is directed toward the recent trend of American higher education to turn to the federal government for advice and leadership. Conant feels that real bedrocks of higher education must be our state legislatures and trustees of private colleges and universities. Up to the present, however, few states have really effectively played a policy-determining role with the real objectives of the institution in mind. California and New York are cited as excellent examples of states which have adopted a system of a master plan in order to effectively plan and coordinate their systems of higher education.

Leach, Richard H. and Redding S. Sugg, Jr. *The Administration of Interstate Compacts.* Baton Rouge, La.: Louisiana State University Press, 1959. 243 pp.

This work gives a detailed explanation of the Interstate Compact— its development, operation, and function. This rather new creature in public administration arose out of the concern for those areas of government which fall by default to the federal government if not occupied by the states. By remaining problem-oriented and through effective cooperation on a regional level, these agencies have made significant contributions in such areas as education, natural resources, and specific public problems.

Levine, Daniel U. "The States Run Scared," *Phi Delta Kappan,* Vol. 47, No. 3, (November, 1965), pp. 134-135.

This article reports on the Kansas City planning conference to implement the State Compact for Education. The tone of the conference was both positive and optimistic toward the compact, which will provide machinery to collect and interpret information, develop proposals for educational financing, etc. The tone was so positive, in fact, that the assembly voted to create a steering committee, to employ staff, select headquarters, and work with the individual states in establishing an Educational Commission of the States.

Longenecker, Herbert E. "Some Implications of the Educational Compact Proposal for Higher Education," *Educational Record,* Vol. 47, No. 1 (Winter, 1966), pp. 106-112.

"Given the present situation and the widespread apprehension and outright dissent almost unanimously expressed by those in higher education who have carefully and thoughtfully examined the implications of the proposed compact, one course of prompt action now seems relevant: states not yet aligned with the compact should be discouraged from joining it."

Orentlicher, Herman T. "The Compact for Education," *AAUP Bulletin,* Vol. 51, No. 5 (December, 1965), pp. 437-446.

A critique on the September 29-30, 1965 conference held for the planning of the Compact for Education in Kansas City, Missouri. The article explains that under the established compact, an "Educational Commission of the States" will be formed to represent a powerful force in the development and effectuation of policy in all areas and aspects of education in this country. The compact itself, plus a summary of it and other related materials prepared by its drafters, is also included.

"School Men Tie Strings to Their Support of Compact," *Nation's Schools,* Vol. 77, No. 1 (January, 1966), p. 67.

Report on an opinion poll concerning the Compact for Education proposed by Dr. James Conant. The compact, which will provide information on educational policy-making, met with 82 percent approval of schoolmen polled, and 16 percent disapproved on grounds that the compact will lend itself to possible bureaucracy.

Spinning, James M. "Has Conant Created an Establishment of One?," *Nation's Schools,* Vol. 75 (January, 1965), pp. 28+.

An article outlining James B. Conant's proposal for a national policy in education. He calls on educators to (1) discredit the accreditation associations for teacher education and certification; (2) to examine our educational needs and performance state by state, through lay committees dedicated to facts; (3) to restructure and strengthen our state education departments; (4) to create voluntary collaboration of the states on "Interstate Commission for Planning a National Educational Policy."

Wayson, W. W. "The Political Revolution in Education, 1965," *Phi Delta Kappan,* Vol. XLVII, No. 7 (March, 1966), pp. 333-339.

The author says that educators should encourage and engage in more and more investigations of our educational policy processes. First, to understand and perhaps direct emerging changes in local, state, and federal roles; second, to develop systematic knowledge about the politics of education upon which to base a training program for future educational statement. The Compact for Education is cited.

Wynn, Richard. "An Inept Lesson in Educational Policy Making," *Phi Delta Kappan,* Vol. XLVII, No. 6 (February, 1966), pp. 251-256.

This is an analysis of Conant's book, *Shaping Educational Policy.* Mr. Wynn suggests that the book is an oversimplified and astonishingly erroneous description of the interaction of governmental and voluntary associations in a few states. His primary quarrel is related to Conant's proposed policy-making at the state level of government.

Section VII

The University and The State—
A Comparative Study

American Council on Education. "Higher Education as a National
Resource," *School & Society,* Vol. 91 (May 4, 1963), pp. 218-
221.

The American Council on Education's proposal for a broad program
of federal action to help expand and improve American education.
The proposal is based on the premise that higher elucation constitutes
a precious national resource essential to the achievement of national
goals and the aspirations of individual citizens.

Anderson, C. Arnold. "Educational Planning in the Context of
National Social Policy," *Phi Delta Kappan,* Vol. XLVII, No. 4
(December, 1965), pp. 180-7.

"Planning is viewed with considerable skepticism, but the main burden and argument will revolve around the ambiguities and dilemmas
arising from efforts to make educational policy depend upon non-
educational ends. Indeed, in my view, the nature of formal education
limits the extent to which it can be profitably assessed in terms of
criteria drawn from outside. Since planning involves choices, as does
policy-making generally, the discussion is organized around a few
basic decisions. . . ."

Benjamin, Harold R. W. *Higher Education in the American Republics.* New York: McGraw-Hill, 1965. 224 pp.

Under the auspices of the Council on Higher Education in the American Republics, the author in this volume has made a major contribution to the area of comparative higher education. The countries of
the American Republics are divided into five regions, each region
comprising a section of the book. Realizing that education is a function of society and that it operates as an integral part of a nation's
culture, the author discusses each nation's educational program in
context with that nation's period of development. Of special note is
chapter nine entitled "Some Future Possibilities" in which the author
draws together significant trends in the twenty-one republics which
will be important between the years 1965-2000.

Bowen, William G. "University Finance in Britain and the United
States: Implications of Financing Arrangements for Educational
Issues," *Public Finance,* Vol. XVIII, No. 1 (1963), pp. 45-83.

The author describes the most striking differences between patterns
of university finance in Britain and the United States, and indicates

some of the implications of these differences for issues of educational policy. He argues for a "many-faced system" of financing higher education in both countries.

Brubacher, John S. *Bases for Policy in Higher Education*: Center for the Study of Higher Education, University of Michigan. New York: McGraw-Hill. 144 pp.

In the author's words, this work is an attempt to "make a more comprehensive or systematic statement of the principles on which education is based." Realizing that higher education is now, more than ever before, being confronted with the question of whether education should be broad or specialized, the author seeks to present a comparative study of different views in regard to this question. He points out that the policies and practices of higher institutions today are too often a product of unconscious forces rather than a consistent philosophy of education.

Committee on Higher Education. *Higher Education.* Report of the Committee appointed by the Prime Minister under the Chairmanship of Lord Robbins. London: Her Majesty's Stationery Office, 1963. Chapter XVII.

See also appendix 4, "Administrative, Financial, and Economic Aspects of Higher Education."

Dobbins, Charles G., Ed. *Higher Education and the Federal Government*: Programs and Problems. Papers presented at the 45th Annual Meeting, Chicago, October, 1962. Washington, D. C.: The American Council on Education, 1963. 127 pp.

A broad coverage of the programs and problems involved in the relationship between higher education and the federal government. Includes remarks by both leaders of government and higher education, which indicated at the time serious problems did exist but were the product of common concerns and could be solved. Select bibliography, pp. 117-26.

Duff, Sir James and Robert O. Berdahl. *University Government in Canada.* Report of a Commission sponsored by the Canadian Association of University Teachers and the Association of Colleges and Universities in Canada. Toronto: University of Toronto Press, 1966.

Dubay, Thomas. *Philosophy of the State as Educator.* Milwaukee, Wisconsin: Bruce Publishing Co., 1959. 231 pp.

The book establishes the position that a state must provide for and maintain its educational system. Mostly a broad, philosophical discussion using the term "state" to mean society or government in general. Deals with topics of natural law, state or educator, and the state's duties toward itself.

Financing Higher Education in Canada: Being the Report of a Committee to the Association of Universities and Colleges of Canada. Toronto: University of Toronto Press, 1965. 98 pp.

A comprehensive, detailed report on ways of financing higher education in Canada. Agreeing with the American trend of recent years, the report emphasizes that every level of government should assume an increased role in meeting the demands of higher education. The economics of higher education in relation to growth, investment, rate of return on investment, and the pricing of higher education are all discussed. In general this volume represents Canada's rationale of how to finance their higher education.

Lee, Dennis S. "Financing Higher Education in the United States and in Great Britain," *Economics of Higher Education*. Office of Education, United States Department of Health, Education, and Welfare. Washington: Government Printing Office, 1962, pp. 328-345.

Establishes that, while the United States and Great Britain will both increase their expenditures in higher education three-fold in the sixties, the means of doing this are different and varied. The author explains that the basic difference in the two governments' expenditures on education is in the amount of student fees the students pay in comparison to government expenditure. In the United States, students assume a larger incidence of the cost through fees than in Britain, resulting in government expenditure comprising less of institution's income in the United States than in Britain. The conclusion is reached that a "loan program for financing student costs" would best benefit both countries in helping their systems maintain academic freedom.

McConnell, T. R. "The Coordination of State Systems of Higher Education," *Emerging Patterns in American Higher Education*, Logan Wilson, Ed. Washington, D. C.: American Council on Education, 1965. pp. 129-141.

The author gives comprehensive coverage to the development and forms of the various state systems of coordination and cooperation in higher education. Areas covered include: Voluntary Systems; The Single Board; The Coordinating Board; Coordinated Planning; and Major Trends in Coordination. Includes select bibliography.

—————. *A General Pattern for American Public Higher Education*. New York: McGraw-Hill, 1962. 198 pp.

Discusses ways in which American colleges and universities can adapt to the "rising tide" of enrollment through state-wide coordination and cooperation. In suggesting such a plan, the diversity of the student and the various demands of our society must be accurately incorporated and represented. It is pointed out that coordination has a constructive role to play in providing both efficiently run schools and schools which optimize a state's given resources.

—————. "A Revolution in British Higher Education?," *NEA Journal*, Vol. 54, No. 5 (May, 1965), pp. 55-6.

Referring to the Lord Robbins Committee on Higher Education, the author indicates that Great Britain is passing through a revolutionary phase—the idea that ". . . courses of higher education should be available for all those who are qualified by ability and attainment to pursue them and who wish to do so." The magnitude of this task is examined by surveying the growth of full-time higher education in Great Britain in this century and by summarizing the expansion proposed by the Robbins Committee.

McGrath, Earl J., Ed. *Universal Higher Education*: Institute of Higher Education. New York: McGraw-Hill, 1966. 247 pp.

Book is comprised of papers presented at the 1964 Institute of Higher Education of which five chapters are pertinent to government and higher education. These are: "Social, Political, Economic, and Personal Consequences" by Henry Steele Commager; "State Systems of Higher Education" by Thomas R. McConnell; "The Impact on Manpower Development and Employment of Youth" by Daniel Patrick Moynihan; "The Economic Aspects" by Algo D. Henderson; "English Higher Education: The Issues Involved" by A.D.C. Peterson; and "Observations and Comments" by Frank H. Bowles. The volume contains a good anthology of material on major issues in higher education.

MacKinnon, Frank. *The Politics of Education*. Toronto, Canada: University of Toronto Press, 1960. 184 pp.

MacKinnon, a Canadian political scientist and educator, explains the inevitable way education is affected by politics and government. His discussion is of both the Canadian and American scene and more generally government and education. Chapter 7 "Control without Dominance" suggests that when government becomes involved in an activity such as education it should "delegate its authority to a body which can act independently of political pressure and departmental routine."

Munger, Frank J. *National Politics and Federal Aid to Education*. Syracuse, N. Y.: Syracuse University Press, 1962. 193 pp.

A factual presentation of the political factors, i.e., interest groups, legislative, government agencies in the problem of getting a program of federal aid to public education passed. Although the work is mostly on public education in general and lacks material since 1962, it does contain some very good descriptions of some political practices which don't meet the eye. Includes bibliography.

National Academy of Sciences. *Basic Research and National Goals*: A Report to the Committee on Science and Astronautics, U. S. House of Representatives. Washington: Government Printing Office, March, 1965. 366 pp.

Composed of a series of articles by leading academicians and scholars, this volume sought to answer two broad questions presented by the House Committee on Science and Astronautics: (1) What level of federal support is needed to maintain for the United States a position of leadership through basic research in the advancement of science and technology and their economic, cultural, and military applications? and (2) What judgment can be reached on the balance of support now being given by the federal government to various fields of scientific endeavor, and on adjustments that should be considered, either within existing levels of support or under conditions of increased or decreased over-all support?

Perkins, James A. "The New Conditions of Autonomy," *Emerging Patterns in American Higher Education,* Logan Wilson, Ed. Washington, D. C.: The American Council on Education, 1965. pp. 8-17.

Within the context of academic freedom and university autonomy, the author discusses the relationships between modern government, industry, and education and the combinations of interests. Specifically covered are: Growth and Specialization; Decentralization and Specialization; Faculty and Administration; State, Regional, and National Organizations; International Agencies; and The Hierarchy of Structures. He concludes that a large degree of autonomy is necessary if the university is to properly perform its function and maintain academic freedom and that this autonomy will depend primarily upon the statesmanship abilities of university administrators.

Peterson, A. D. C. "English Higher Education: The Issues Involved," *Universal Higher Education,* Earl McGrath, Ed. New York: McGraw-Hill, 1966, pp. 218-34.

Reuther, Walter D. "The Challenge to Education in a Changing World," *Education and the Public Good.* Cambridge, Mass.: Harvard University Press, 1964.

A discourse on the challenge our nation's higher education must accept as a free nation. Stresses the interdependence of education and government in satisfying our chronic need for a unified effort in the area of education.

Riesman, David. *Constraint and Variety in American Education.* Lincoln, Nebraska: University of Nebraska Press, 1965. 160 pp.

The author has attempted to place American higher education in its cultural context. The book is divided into three sections each concerned with a separate focus of attention. "The Academic Procession" portrays the opposing forces and directions shaping educational curriculum. In the second on "The Intellectual Veto Groups" he presents the interdisciplinary collaboration of newer social sciences as veto groups. In his last chapter he deals with the role of secondary education in our system.

——————. "Notes on New Universities: British and American," *Universities Quarterly,* Vol. 21 (March, 1966), pp. 128-46.

". . . as an American, I feel that the new British universities as well as innovative stirrings in the older ones can be important on a trans-Atlantic basis. I hope the experiments are not abandoned because of the work they entail, the emotional wear and tear. Yet I recognize that an experiment which even in part succeeds runs an inevitable risk. . . ."

Ross, Murray G. "The President's Report." Excerpts from *These Five Years*. Toronto, Canada: York University, 1965. pp. 24-31.

Ross, former president of the new York University in Toronto, proposes a rapid expansion of that university but he wants to retain the colleges system in an effort toward personal education. The first of the twelve residential colleges is now complete on the still raw campus. The York plan is to build one college for each 1,000 students and to expand at the rate of one campus a year.

Sufrin, Sidney C. *Issues in Federal Aid to Education*. Syracuse, N. Y.: Syracuse University Press, 1962.

Although primarily oriented to elementary and secondary education, the author develops the idea that federal aid to education is indicative of a national interest in education. However, the assertion of a national interest demands more than federal funds; it must also include goals and standards and a new pattern of relationships between and among the various levels of governments and private parties concerned with public education. Calls for expanded functions of the United States Office of Education. Includes index and bibliographical notes.

Trytten, M. H. "Higher Education as an Instrument of National Policy," *Current Issues in Higher Education,* G. Kerry Smith, Ed. The Proceedings of the Fourteenth Annual National Conference on Higher Education, Chicago, March, 1959. Washington, D. C.: Association for Higher Education, 1959.

The author contends that the educational process serves the nation best when it is true unto itself, but "only if there is a genuine awareness of national needs, and a willingness to meet those needs with initiative and imagination."

United States Congress, House Committee on Government Operations, Subcommittee on Research and Programs. *Conflicts between the Federal Research Programs and the Nation's Goals for Higher Education*. 89th Congress, 1st Session. Washington: Government Printing Office, 1965. 114 pp.

This publication provides a valuable look at this pressing question. It is made up of the responses of the academic and other interested communities to an inquiry by Congress. Includes excerpts and replies from some of the 300 persons polled. Questions were asked of the students, faculty, institutions, graduates, and the government.

Venables, Sir Peter. "Confusion, Concentration and Clarification in Higher Education," *Comparative Education,* Vol. 2 (November, 1963), pp. 11-18.

————————. "Dualism in Higher Education," *Universities Quarterly,* Vol. 20 (December, 1965), pp. 16-29.

"The administrative means to maintain the academic well being of both universities and colleges need also to be considered critically and constructively. It will be a far ranging and searching debate including many matters . . . not yet touched upon. . . ."

Wilson, Logan. "Basic Premises for a National Policy in Higher Education," *Emerging Patterns in American Higher Education,* Logan Wilson, Ed. Washington, D. C.: American Council on Education, 1965, pp. 263-271.

Believing that a national policy for higher education is essential to our nation's welfare, the author sets down eight "premises or guidelines" upon which such a policy should be based. In order to establish such a policy a shift from independence to interdependence is fundamental in each of the eight suggestions. Emphasis is made to the point that a national policy does not or should not mean necessarily a total federally initiated coordination. Freedom still must play an important part in determining the proper mixture of diversity and coordination.

————————. "A Better Partnership for the Federal Government and Higher Education," *Emerging Patterns in American Higher Education,* Logan Wilson, Ed. Washington, D. C.: American Council on Education, 1965, pp. 272-281.

In this article Logan Wilson suggests certain major principles which should be sought in developing the ideal "partnership" between the federal government and higher education. He sets forth six such principles, ranging from the broad, encompassing one of allocating funds as to national interest and not regional pressure, to more concise principles such as the selectivity and merit qualifications of allocating federal programs.

————————. "Myths and Realities of Institutional Independence," *Emerging Patterns in American Higher Education,* Logan Wilson, Ed. Washington, D. C.: American Council on Education, 1965, pp. 18-28.

In this article the author addresses himself to the problem of what is a "proper" or "improper" constraint on an institution's independence. By tracing past traditions of institutional autonomy and present influences on this autonomy, the author suggests that we can no longer reject the idea that our colleges and universities operate in a highly interdependent era which is becoming more "politicized" every year. In conclusion, Wilson feels university organization and administration has lacked the concentrated reorganization and change which industry and government have long been experiencing.

Wilson, Logan, Ed. *Emerging Patterns in American Higher Education.* A collection of essays. Washington, D. C.: American Council on Education, 1965. 292 pp.

This volume of essays is contributed by the nation's leading educators and scholars; it is a comprehensive overview of American higher education today. Directed primarily at organization and direction, it covers: the changing environment of higher education; institutional modifications; the emergence of state systems; voluntary arrangements; interinstitutional and interstate agreements; unified approaches to national problems; national associations in higher education; and national policy for higher education: problems and prospects. Primary emphasis is toward the emergence of a stronger national higher educational policy.